THE KANAKHALA CONNECTION

A Case of Divine Mysticism

Debabrata Maulik

INDIA • SINGAPORE • MALAYSIA

Made with ❤ on the Notion Press Platform

www.notionpress.com

Handing over the book with pleasure to my wife and son who have been my constant companions in my tryst with Divine Mysticism

Contents

Part I

Part II

Prelude

Human thoughts are two way traffics. Thoughts of self-centric nature set up communication with extra terrestrial power, while thoughts directed outward produce wonders outside.

When some being or a hero performs or an event occurs particularly concerned with a deity or a demigod, who cannot be determined on the basis of a fact or a natural explanation it is termed a legend or a legendary story. Traditional wisdom explains it to be some practice, rite or phenomenon of nature. This legendary story is long considered as a Myth. The Study and collated presentation of myths constitutes what is known as Mythology.

It is often said Mythology plays important role in laying the foundation for a practising religion. Traditionally there are three types of Myth. Aetiological (etiological) Myth explains the reason why something is the way it is today; Historical Myth tells about a historical event and help keeping its memory alive. The third one is Psychological Myth.

In the primitive stages of survival of mankind on the earth human life feels the existence of an unknown power in their ambient. Inquisition to know about that power evokes their rational instinct. A process of communications develops between them and the unknown power. Initially that remains unidirectional in the form of uttering. The uttering of slokas gets transmitted as Srutis down the generation. Much later developed the written down words and symbols of communication.

As civilisation progresses human being lives on traditions. The traditions guide their cultures and characters. Such traditions in the early human civilization give rise to many narratives and texts. Hindu literatures viz., Vedas and Upanishads, the epics like Mahabharata and Ramayana, the Puranas carries them. Since then these texts become integral part of Hindus life. That is when mythology takes its root and binds all these texts in one common thread of faith and belief.

Using myths and mythology Epics have interwoven contrast characters, the good against the evil, the honest against the dishonest, the dharma-bound lover against the anti-dharma bully, and the gentle and compassionate against the cruel and greedy. Puranas use myths and mythology to tell the history of the Universe from creation to destruction. Epics integrate in a wide range of subjects, viz. origin of cosmos, humans or all life forms originated (anthropogony), origin of gods (theogony). Puranas provide the genealogies of kings, heroes, sages, deities, cosmology, geography and philosophy in a simpler manner to popularize the thoughts of the Vedas among the ordinary people.

Traditionally 18 principle Puranas emerged in three phases 350 – 750 CE, 750 – 1000 CE and 1000 – 1500 CE. Composed primarily in Sanskrit many of the Puranas are named after major Hindu deities such as Vishnu, Shiva, Brahmadev and Shakti.

A portion of the Markandeya Purana is well known to Hindus as Chandi, or Devimahatmya. Worship of God as the Divine Mother is its theme. Myths and mythologies associated with the Divine Mother make Divine events go deep in the heart of Hindus. One such event leads to create the Abode of Divine Mother Goddess Adi Shakti on the Earth.

Ж Ψ Φ Ω ↂ

Author's Comment

"In the guise of service to mankind a despot uses power to glorify self-personage. Continuous indulgence of such disgraceful condemnable acts brings in catastrophic end of the world"

The Universe or the Cosmos is governed by many rules integrated in system itself by its creation. Since ancient time human beings at various stages of evolutionary progresses have been able to understand only a part of its mystery. Deep in the mystery of Universe, human beings are first stirred by the thunderbolts accompanied with lightening. They are struck with wonder in experiencing the tornado, great power of wind storms. They are shuddered by the power of the tsunami, the vast power of water bodies like oceans, Rivers, etc. causing ravages of destruction. They experience the cycle of daylight and darkness of the night, occurring of eclipses and many other such cosmological events. Such events might have forced them to ponder on these cosmic phenomena. With the development of human intellect those phenomena have led the practising scientists, physicist, engineers and scholars to search for answers. In the Indian context practising scholars' viz., the Sages, Rishis, Spiritual Teachers, etc. extrapolates their knowledge mixed with the wings of imaginations for the matters starting from creation of the Universe to the smallest happenings in early life.

Hindus claim that knowledge of the Universe is parted first time by the Vedic Sages. Early literatures viz, the Vedas, Upanishads and Puranas provide the basis of future perusal of studies on the universe. Hindus has spirituality associated a human symbolism or personage with every cosmological function. These lead to creation of idol or deity for further propagation of knowledge among the common people. Through the idols or deities people start indulging in communicating with extra terrestrial existence.

Extrapolation thereon consequently brings in the concept of the Supreme Being as the Primordial Inconceivable Energy. To Hindus the unknown energy in the super condensed form which has emitted the first blasting light is the Primordial Inconceivable Energy. Their spiritual vibration visualises this great energy in the form of metaphor as the Mother of creation. Hindus name her as Goddess Adi Parashakti or Adi Shakti. Primordial Source of Energy lies in the Dark unknown Space. Hindus believe that the entire event of creations has the common source of power of a female origin. Female power in combination with male foresightedness and wisdom is considered as the source of 'Shakti' or 'Power'. The explanation of the Supreme Being as the Goddess Adi Parashakti or Adi Shakti described in Part I enable us understanding the Shakti mythology also. Hindus consider a Shaktipeeth with great reverence as the Center of Divine Energy on the earth for worshipping of Goddess Adi Shakti.

A place on the Earth named Kanakhala near Haridwar used to echo sacrificial hymns uttered by the Holi Sages throughout the year. Long ago in the Satya Yuga there occurs a Divine event. Divine events when followed in a semi-fictional way finds many a time intrigued with the strange characters and their roles. Mythological characters and their roles as mentioned in the Puranas when explored in a semi-fictional scanner give rise to taking the natural inquisition of the readers travel along these characters in an investigative manner. One becomes eager to know the conclusion at the earliest. Anonymous acts leads to the opening up of the playground and to the climax of the Divine event concluded in the Part I.

Years' later humans engage in roaming amidst these Divine Centers on the Earth in search of the divine connection. The travelogue in Part II brings in this aspect through 19 sub-sections. In reality the travelogue is the outcome of author's personal visits to the Shaktipeeths encountering their mysticism. These visits have showcased the enormous faith Hindus carry for Goddess Adi Shakti. It has validated the truth that worshipping Adi Shakti in the Divine Energy Centres known as Shaktipeeths has remained eternally close to the Hindus. A very few of other Hindu temples is guarded with so much mystery as that of a Shaktipeeth.

"Sarva Mangala Mangalye Sive Sarvartha Sadhike Saranye Trayambike Gauri Narayani Namostute"

Ж Ψ Φ Ω ↂ

Rising of Early Human Intellect ~India Story

It is often felt that there exist voids in our learning of the progressive history of human advancement. Amongst many the one pertains to the period of the rising of early human intellect. A brief account of the progressive history of human, the India story offers an interesting chapter.

Present day human beings are developed on earth by the process of human evolution from now-extinct primates. It is zoologically viewed that a culture-bearing upright-walking species that lives on the ground and very likely first evolved in about 315,000 years ago. Grouped generally as Homo sapiens (first to use some form of language) their evolution begins from archaic humans 300,000-150,000 years ago primarily in east Africa. Passing through time they become capable of migrating to new destinations independently. Some migrates to the Southwest Asia around 100000 years ago and some to elsewhere in the Old World by 60,000-40,000 years ago during a short temperate period in the midst of the last ice age.

The first primitive habitants in the Indian sub-continent comprise of among others descendants of the out of Africa migrants during 65000 years ago. Zagrosian herders also have migrated to India between 7000 and 3000 BCE. They are the first to goat domestication. Together, they go to create the Harappan civilisation in the North West part of the Indian sub-continent sometime between 5000 and 4500 BCE. The civilisation reaches its zenith between 2300 and 2000 BCE.

It is not exactly known when humans first became religious. But there is credible archeological evidence of religious-cum-ritualistic behavior from around the Middle Paleolithic era (45 – 200 thousand years ago).

In the Indian context human life evolves from small hunter-gatherer tribes into large agrarian cultures. They have needed to encourage co-operation and tolerance among relative strangers. This challenge leads to the development of a common medium driven by the belief in a moralizing Guide what is known as Religion. It is a cultural adaptation to those challenges. The evolution of religious beliefs and behaviors in those early modern humans develop seven traits. They are animism, belief in an afterlife, shamanism (a religious practice that involves a practitioner interacting with what they believe to be a spirit world through altered states of consciousness, such as trance which is a state of semi-consciousness, with the goal of directing spirits or spiritual energies into the physical world for the purpose of healing, divination or to aid human beings in some other way), ancestor worship, high gods, and worship of ancestors or high gods.

Second set of immigrants from the Eurasian Steppe, probably from the Central Asian region arrive in the Indus Valley in the centuries after 2000 BCE. They are said to have brought with them an early version of Sanskrit, mastery over horses and a range of new cultural practices such as sacrificial rituals, yajna, etc. They are called Indo-Aryans.

Natural curiosity arises in human beings and encounters with the embedded power in the natural calamities and cosmic events.

The idea that a supremely great and powerful being exist or ever did exist starts haunting them. After ensuring safety and security first, both the old and new habitants adapt and practice various means (including worshipping as they believe) simultaneously to satisfy the unknown supremely great authority. Mixed community collectively names the moralizing Guide as God. People turned to believe in the one all – pervasive God who energies the entire universe. Belief grow among them that God is both in the world and beyond it. This belief system is first set down in writing in the works known as the Vedas during the so-called Vedic Period 1500 – 500 BCE but the concepts have been transmitted through generations orally long before. The propagation of the eternal knowledge is known as *shruti* ("what is heard") and is set down in the Vedas and their various sections.

This form of the belief system, often termed as Vedism developed by the Vedic people leads to the foundation of a new theological system in the Indus Valley prior to the 3rd century BCE. The belief system of the Vedic people composed in Sanskrit has produced the Vedas. The Vedas seek to understand the nature of existence and the individual's place in the cosmic order. In pursuing these questions, the sages create that highly developed theological system, which become known as Hinduism and people involved in developing this system are celled Hindus.

Human thoughts go on rapid honing. Above works are further complemented by another type of communication known as smritis ("what is remembered") which relates stories on how one is to practice the faith. All these developments said to have taken place between 5th to 3rd centuries BCE. The outcomes are the Puranas, the epics – Mahabharata and Ramayana, the Yoga Sutras and the Bhagavad Gita. They are the revelation of the truth of existence which claims the universe is rational, structured, and controlled by the Supreme Being, conceptualised as Brahman in whose essence all human beings take part. Vedic concept of the Supreme Being as Brahman is created.

Human beliefs are on many gods in the pantheon of Vedism who could have been looked to as the First Cause. But the sages go beyond the anthropomorphic deities and recognize that "there is wholeness, an undivided reality that is more fundamental than being or non-being". This entity is envisioned as an individual but one so great and powerful as to be beyond all human comprehension. This Being they come to refer to as Brahman does not just exist in reality (another being like any others) nor outside of reality (in the realm of non-being or pre-existence) but is actual reality itself. Brahman not only causes things to be as they are; it is things as they are, has always been, and will always be.

From 1500 BCE onwards fusion of the language and culture of the Indo-Aryans with the indigenous local people of the region enables the beliefs and practices of the Vedas, a collection of hymns to be complied and lead to the development of what is known as Hinduism. The term Hinduism is more of an exonym (a name given by others to a people, place, or concept). It is presumed to have derived from the name Sindus (pronunciation of S as H) designating those who lived across the Indus River. Most scholars believe Hinduism have started somewhere between 15th and 5th century BCE in the Indus Valley. The first and foremost reason being the belief in the Vedas – that grew through four texts compiled between the 15th and 5th centuries BCE and the faith's belief in Brahman, the Supreme Being from whom all of creation emerges. Brahman is the First Cause which sets all else in motion but is also that which is in motion, that which guides the course of creation, and creation itself. While Vedism has conceptualised Brahman as the Supreme Being, Hinduism gives the freedom to approach God in one's own way, encouraging a multiplicity of paths, not asking for conformity to just one. Thus unlike other religions, Hinduism has no one founder but is instead a fusion of various beliefs.

Humans have the same basic brain. Religious belief set the path to modern life by promoting the social good. Evidence for God's existence is widely felt in the creation, conscience, rationality and experience. Sharpen intellect of the human mind produces the Epic, Puranic and Classics in the periods between 5th century BCE and 5th century AD. Hindus begin to emphasize the worship of deities, especially Vishnu, Shiva and Devi. By 3rd century BCE knowledge and art of sculpture has been established in India by the Maurya Empire period and by early 1st century BCE, the term murti (meaning idols, image or statue) have appeared in various Indian texts. First humans in the Indian soil are gradually elevated to the next higher level.

Elevation of the first human gave birth to the earliest roots of Indian astronomy that dated to the period of Indus Valley civilisation or earlier. Astronomy developed as a discipline of the Vedas dating 1400 – 600 BCE, gave some cosmological concepts as notions of the movement of heavenly bodies and the course of the year. Rig Veda, the oldest one describes time as a wheel with 12 parts and 360 spokes (days), with a remainder of 5, making reference to the solar calendar. Indian astronomy flowered in the 5th–6th century AD, with Aryabhatta, whose work covered topics such as units of time, methods for determining the positions of planets, the cause of day and night, and several other cosmological concepts. The text today known as *Surya Siddhanta* dates to the Gupta period and was perceived by Aryabhatta. Other astronomers of the classical era who further elaborated on Aryabhatta work include Brahmagupta, Varahamihira and Lalla. An identifiable native Indian astronomical tradition remained active throughout the medieval period and into the 16th or 17th century.

Human intellect rises to create early cosmology too in Hinduism as found in Rig Veda. There is mention that the universe is very old but it is not clear where it came from or when it began. Hindus believe that there are many universes floating around in space as well as floating of many different ideas about its creation. Ideas consist that time goes around in a cycle and that it is continually destroyed and recreated. Each cycle of time is termed as a Yuga. Hindus also believe that there is spirit and matter, which are different realities. Spirit is known as Purusha (the male component) and matter is known as Prakriti (the female component).

Rising human intellect next added the Puranas, present an elaborate mythical cosmography of the universe. Universe consists of three levels — heaven, earth, and the netherworld. Earth, the middle level consists of seven circular continents. The central one surrounded by the salty ocean and each of the other concentric continents by oceans. In the centre of the central mainland stands the cosmic mountain Meru; the southernmost portion of this mainland is Bharatavarsa, the old name for India. Above earth there are seven layers in heaven, at the summit of which is the world of Brahman (Brahmaloka); there are also seven layers below earth, the location of hells inhabited by serpents and demons.

The story of the first human in the Indian sub-continent thus covers a long path from being a small hunter-gatherer (5000 BCE) to become the great Sages and Scholars of Hinduism (5th century AD). Human evolution undergoes perfecting their brain power over these years. Development of the Vedas, Hinduism, the idea of an all powerful God, the Hindu astronomy, time and universe and cosmology, Puranas, Epic, idea of spirit, matter and creation wrapped with occasional mythological essence are the outcomes. The original ideas become the foundation of Hindu's scholarly contributions to the world of science. India's religious perception gets founded on a strong note and enhanced for mass consumption through mythological wrap and flourishes in the subsequent centuries in the medieval India.

Great Sages and Scholars resort to the mythological swathe in describing the Divine events. Motivated Human with their growing intellect continues to wander in search of the Brahman, the Supreme Being even today and trying to explore its existence on the earth.

The sole purpose of constructing the above texts is to easy our understanding of the inner thoughts of the progressive rising intellect of our early ancestors. With all humility I acknowledge that above expression (howsoever deficient it may be) is entirely mine and personal and in no way aims to hurt any soul.

ЖΨΦΩↂ

Part I

The Kanakhala Mystery

Many years ago there used to be a small colony of people located on the foothills of the Himalaya. It is a village in the southern part of the present day Haridwar district of Uttarakhand. Its name used to be Kanakhala. In later days it becomes known as Kankhal. This is the place where Holy Ganges descends on the plain. Presence of the Ganges makes it a holy and an auspicious place to the ancient sages. It is said Vedic Sages used to perform their spiritual acts and sacrifices on the banks of the holy river. The place used to remain filled with Sanskrit hymns. It is believed to be the second home of Shiva.

After creating the basic concept of time Brahmadev provides through his mind-sons and Sages and Rishis the concept of four Yugas viz. Satya, Treta, Dwapar and Kali. In the Satyayuga (also known as Kritayuga) characterised by gigantic, big-built, virtuous, honest and righteous human beings living for thousands of years, a Divine event happens. Hindu Puranas wrapped in mythology has mention of it. The secrets of the event involve celestial characters and comprise the Kanakhala mystery for many years. The mysterious event is believed to have sown the seed of a Divine Connection.

Chapter 1

Appearance of the Operator

The Operator walks through the flower-filled garden located on Mount Meru, signifying only the absolute reality of infinite Pure Consciousness-Bliss, the highest of the joyful worlds a person might attain.

It is the Satyaloka the abode of the Operator and his consort.

There are lotus flowers everywhere in the Brahmaloka. These lotuses are huge, with divine energy flowing out of them. In the center of Satyaloka is Brahmapura, a huge palace in which the Operator lives in.

Below Satyaloka is Tapaloka and above it are the end of the material universe and the start of the Vaikunth planets.

The Operator, the vivifying expansive force of nature in its eternally periodic Manvantara, stands for the spiritual evolving or developing energy-consciousness of a solar system of Brahmanda, signifying the Operator as Brahmadev.

But what is this vivifying expansive force that provides energy consciousness. Scholarly human mind has explored this vivifying unrestrained force taking in a personified form through the passage of time.

Billions of years ago in the sudden shaking of the vast unknown dark space time starts for the very first time. At the beginning the space has been very hot and small. Since then it has been in the continuous mode of expansion and simultaneous cooling down.

After the lapse of about billion years water appears and occupies much of the expanse of the Universe. Water is termed Nara in Sanskrit and ayana means a bed. The unending expanse of water bed prompts scholars to name it Narayana. Hindus consider this as abode of Vishnu.

All the life forms have appeared from water in the beginning – is scientific fact. Without water molecules life forms cannot originate.

One school of thoughts come in to suggest that a life is created on its own from the primeval waters as a seed inside a Golden egg or the Golden embryo. Spiritual scholars have visualised the appearance of the golden egg by the act of the same dynamic force i.e. the Primordial Inconceivable Energy which held in the Golden Womb (Hiranyagarbha). This is the source of the creation of universe or the manifested cosmos in Vedic philosophy.

Golden egg grew over a very long period. Upanishad calls it the Soul of the universe or Brahman and elaborate that Hiranyagarbha floated around in the emptiness and the darkness of the non-existence for about one whole gods-year (1 Deva-Vatsara = 129600 human years) along with the life lived inside the Golden egg. The Golden embryo egg keeps on growing. In Sanskrit word "Brih" means "'to grow" or "to expand." In this way, growing Golden egg or the Golden embryo becomes synonymous with the word Brahma. From the growing Golden Egg the life inside draws the name Brahma (or Brahmadev). The golden egg grew big and then split into two halves. The two halves of the shell became heaven and earth, within which Brahmadev fashioned the sky as modern science compared it with principle of Big Bang theory where it is considered that world is emerged from a single point. Creation of sky, directions, time, language and senses follow both in heaven and earth. This way the Golden egg gives rise to the Brahmanda and the life created therein is Brahmadev, the Operator.

ЖΨΦΩↀ

The origins of the term Brahma are uncertain. There are several related words found in the Vedic literature, such as Brahman for the 'Ultimate Reality' and Brahmana for 'priest'. A distinction between the spiritual concept of Brahman and the deity Brahma is that the former neuter form is a genderless abstract metaphysical concept in Hinduism while the latter is one of the many masculine gods in Hindu tradition. The spiritual concept of Brahman is quite old and some scholars suggest that the deity Brahma may have emerged as a personification and visible icon of the impersonal universal principle Brahman. The existence of a distinct deity named Brahma is evidenced in late Vedic texts.

Grammatically, the nominal stem Brahma – has two distinct forms: the neuter noun Brahman, whose nominative singular form is Brahma; and the masculine noun Brahman, whose nominative singular form is Brahma. The former, He is one of the members of the Hindu trinity and associated with creation, but does not have a cult in present-day India. This is because Brahma, the creator-god, is long-lived but not eternal i.e. Brahma gets absorbed back into Purusha at the end of an aeon, and is born again at the beginning of a new kalpa.

Puranas has portrayed Brahmadev as the one who rises from the "Ocean of Causes". They mention Brahmadev emerges at the moment when time and universe is born, inside a lotus rooted in the navel of Narayan (ocean bed of water).

Brahma's emergence from the navel lotus of Narayana is allegorically comparable as the principle of creation of all manifest realms – its laws, its inherent intelligence, and it's consciously manifested potencies which operate as Sages, Saints, Rishis, Devas, Celestials, and Divine beings of all kinds of nature, temperament and description for trillions of years, then dissolves back into Narayana. Later another Brahmadev appears to begin the process again.

So Brahmadev appears as the principle operator of the universe while Narayana stands to mean the sum and substance of all the manifested and unmanifested realms.

Operator godhead Brahmadev's is a very complex story. Hindus believe in the multifaceted Brahmadev as the God of Creation and Evolution, the God of Cosmology, God of Astronomy, God of Mathematics. Unlike Vishnu or Shiva or Adi Shakti, Brahmadev has a self-created existence as commonly believed.

In the beginning Brahmadev has the drowsy, erring and incompetent form. But soon he becomes aware of his confusion and drowsiness inner urge motivates him to meditate as an ascetic. Soon he sees the beginning and end of universe and then his creative powers are revived. The Operator is casted.

The Operator spends alone in isolation for a very long period.

Then He tries to engage in the creation of living beings in the universe. His each move involves in the whole transformation of creation when the Cosmic Super Energy change from 'Nirakar' ('Formless') to 'Sakar' (acquired 'Form').

Very early from the Operator, continuing to meditate, are born mind-engendered progeny called Manas-putra (mind-sons), with forms and faculties derived from his corporeal nature; embodied spirits, produced from the person of that all-wise deity.

First four Manasputra named Sanaka, Sanatana, Sanandana and Sanatkumara created initially refuses to assist Brahmadev in his creation process and proceed to be in Bramhacharya forever.

So the operator becomes handicapped and worried.

He is not able to comprehend what more will be needed. His process of creation takes a temporary halt.

ЖΨΦΩↂ

Chapter 2

Operator Comprehends

Clueless Operator becomes engrossed in deep thoughts.

Sometimes pass by, he remembers about the primordial inconceivable energy of the cosmos. He decides to acquaint with it.

He goes in to introspection and gets deeply absorbed in thoughts about this Divine energy. His pure consciousness and knowledge helps in comprehending about all the qualities that merged into conceptualizing what is known as the Supreme Being.

He remembers that in the beginning there has neither existence nor non-existence; there has no atmosphere, no sky and no realm beyond. There has nothing to distinguish night from day. There has no wind or breath. There has nothing perceivable. The darkness has swathed in darkness, only the dark great space or void is present in the beginning. All the unknown energy of the unending space is concentrated to a point in super condensed form. Along the dark endless horizon suddenly there arises a huge expression of a fire with a big knock. A bright light emerges from this point. Then (from when the journey of time starts) there is a sudden vigorous shaking of the space (13.7 billion years ago) and the energy starts spreading and forcing the space to expand continuously. The spreading energy creates all astral things that we see in what constitute the universe. The unknown energy in the super condensed form which emitted the first light is conceived as the Primordial Inconceivable Energy.

Brahmadev updates himself about this primordial cosmic energy which has the ability to move the great dark space to initiate process of building the universe. The energy of the dark space in super concentrated form is the starting point for creation of the universes. The spiritual vibration visualises this great energy in the form of metaphor of feminine dispense as the Mother of creation or the Divine Mother. Hindu scholars name her as Goddess Adi Parashakti or commonly Adi Shakti or simply Shakti.

Long after, the present day advanced science has reached a concept more or less in the similar line.

In respect of the 'Cosmic Power' of the Universe this divine power is named as Adi Parashakti; in respect of the 'Ancient Power' of Planet Earth this divine power is named as the Adi Shakti and in respect of the 'Power' or 'True Nature' of the Earth this divine power is termed as Shakti. Traditionally all these have merged into one belief that is Divine Mother Mahadevi or popularly Adi Shakti.

Brahmadev realises that the enormous water body from which the Golden Egg and the whole world (Brahmanda) wherefrom has emerged, is held in its place by the dynamic force emerged from the same super condensed point where entire energy of the vast unknown dark space is centralised. This is what is termed as Primordial Inconceivable Energy. Creation of the universe is the visible act of this energy which is visualised by the rising intellect of the newly born human in the female form of Mahadevi or Adi Parashakti or commonly the Adi Shakti, the Supreme Being.

Ж Ψ Φ Ω ⊕

The true form of Adi Shakti is unknown, perhaps beyond human comprehension. She is seen as *Anaadi-Ananta* (meaning with no beginning, no ending) and *Nitya* (forever) "The Great Divine Mother" in Hinduism. Energy is seen in all forms all around us. Everything is just a manifestation of energy, but what exactly energy is, no one knows. Energy is the greatest delusion which is termed by Hindus as *Mahamaya*. Divine Mother is thus Mahamaya, a metaphor of energy, which no layman or scientist has ever been able to decipher.

Brahmadev realises that the dynamic forces of the primordial cosmic energy that move through the entire universe are recognised as the Supreme Mother Goddess Adi Parashakti. On every plane of creation, this energy manifests itself in all forms of matter, thermal energy, potential energy, gravitational energy, centrifugal energy, kinetic energy, etc. These are all considered as the infinite forms of the Adi Parashakti. The Primordial Inconceivable Energy in the great creative light that emerged in the beginning is further mystified in following Hindu metaphor as if:

"She had three eyes, hands carrying Trishul, shield, mace, bow, arrow, chakra, long sword and right hand as Abhaya mudra. She looked here and there but saw nothing. After seeing nothing she took the form of Kushmanda. She was seated on a lioness. When she opened her left eye Mahakali was born. When she opened her third eye Mahasaraswati was born and when she opened her right eye Mahalakshmi was born. Before she opened her eyes she smiled a bit and from the smile, all universes were created".

Brahmadev becomes well aware of the Divine Mother Mahadevi or Adi Shakti who is born and become embedded in the psyche of the mankind. He realises that the conceptual fact of Goddess Adi Shakti or Mahadevi is true and comes to stay as the spiritual backbone of the mankind.

ЖΨΦΩↂ

Brahmadev further remembers Adi Shakti's form of Kali as the personification of the Dark Energy, which exists even after the destruction and before the creation of the universe. This energy is also called Zero Energy or Sacred Energy as it is conceived as the truly supreme spirit without form (i.e. Param Atman). Adi Parashakti as Divine Pure Eternal Consciousness i.e. Shoonya Bindu, the divine zero feminine energy then expresses itself as Parama Prakriti (Universal Nature). Since Adi Parashakti is the Param Atman and Parama Prakriti She stands as the mother of all worlds. Both real and unreal, Mahadevi or Adi Shakti is the supreme source who creates and in the end resolves all creation into herself.

Brahmadev further realises Adi Shakti as the energy of the cosmos and the "Eternally Limitless Power" and thus the creator of the universe having neither beginning nor end; she is the only victor and the manifestation of victory itself; she is the only eternal truth; she is the manifested (Brahmadev), un-manifested (Vishnu) and transcendent (Shiva) divinity. She then displays her scarcely seen form: Satyaloka is located in her forehead; the created universe are her hairs; the sun and moon are her eyes; in her ears are the four cardinal directions; the Vedas are her words; death, affection and emotion are her teeth; maya is manifested by her smile.

Brahmadev recognises Adi Shakti to be the Universal Being. She is said to be the Mother of all, to pervade the three worlds, to be the support of all, to be the life force of all beings, to be the ruler of all beings, to be the only cause of the universe, to create Brahmadev, Vishnu, and Siva and to command them to perform their cosmic tasks, to be the root of the tree of the universe, and to be she who is supreme knowledge and positioned cosmic supremacy.

Ж Ψ Φ Ω ↂ

In the belief of the followers of Adi Shakti either Vishnu or Brahmadev is not the cause of the manifestation. If Brahmadev is said to have arisen from the navel of Vishnu and Vishnu himself rests on a thousand hooded serpents which in turn rests on waters, then Vishnu cannot be the highest supreme self. This is because he, the serpent and the waters need another support to stay in place. That support is the same primordial inconceivable energy conceived as Adi Parashakti.

Devi Suktam hymn in Sanskrit of the Rig Veda describes this feminine aspect of God. On conversion in to English it says as follows:

> *"I am Manifested Divinity, Unmanifested Divinity and Transcendent Divinity. I am Brahmadev, Vishnu, and Shiva, as well as Saraswati, Lakshmi, and Parvati. I am the Sun and I am the Stars, and I am also the Moon. I am all animals and birds, and I am the outcast as well, and the thief. I am the low person of dreadful deeds and the great person of excellent deeds. I am Female; I am Male in the form of Shiva."*
>
> **– *Devi-Bhagavata Purana***

In the Srimad Devi Bhagwat Purana Devi Adi Shakti addresses Trimurti, on conversion it reads as follows:

"I am Adi Parashakti, goddess Bhuvaneshwari. I am the owner of this universe. I am the Absolute Reality. I am dynamic in feminine form and static in masculine form. You have appeared to govern the universe through my energy. You are the masculine form of Absolute

Reality, while I am the feminine form of that Reality. I am beyond form, beyond everything, and all the powers of God are contained within me. You must know that I am the Eternal limitless energy".

She then *says "Brahmadev! You will be generator of the universe; the Goddess Sharada (Saraswati) is your consort, my form by which I will be recognized as the goddess of wisdom and the primeval sound. Brahmadev, this goddess will be with you when you create the universe".*

"Narayana! You are the Supreme, Immortal Spirit. You are formless, yet you take form. I assign you to be the preserver of the universe. You will take different incarnations in order to save this universe's inhabitants" She continues.

"Oh Narayana, You are the Supreme of all the deities with form. You have created Brahmadev, and Brahmadev will further create thirty three kinds of gods and goddesses. My Great Power, goddess Mahalaxshmi, has been born from your mystic sleep. You are the Paramatman. Your consort will be goddess Maha Lakshmi, my form. Vishnu, this goddess will be with you when you rule and maintain the universe. When life evolves, you will take the form of Vishnu, the one who will perform the task of observing and preserving this universe" – She completes her address.

Finally She instructs Shiva – *"Oh Rudra, the Great, you are the personification of time, which is above all. You will perform the task of destroying and regenerating this universe.*

When you are formless absolute, time stands still. It is due to my power that you become dynamic and are capable of bringing about the destruction and regeneration of this universe.

Your consort is goddess Mahakali, Mahakali is myself, my full form, where Lakshmi and Saraswati just my clone, partial form. But due to meditation, you will surpass all my forms. It is then that I will incarnate from your left half in my manifested form. This form will be my truest manifested form. She will perform the task of destroying evil and will be your consort."

ЖΨΦΩↀ

Adi Shakti devolves herself to Durga or Parvati (as Material Shakti), Kali (as Vidya Shakti) and Yog Maya (as Mayashakti). As Vidya Shakti she splits herself to 10 kinds of eternal knowledge, known as 10 Mahavidyas represented by ten wisdom goddesses. As per tantras these ten goddesses are original source of ten incarnation of Vishnu. (Source: *Sri Devi Bhagwat Mahapurana*)

Divine Mother Adi Parashakti in her manifestation as Goddess Durga controls the nine planets and stars in nine different forms to maintain the cosmic orders of the universe. These Nav Durga forms are: *Kushmanda Shakti* governing the Sun; *Mahagauri* governing the Rahu; *Kaal Ratri* governs the Shani; *Siddhi Dhatri* governing the Ketu; *Katyayini* governing the Brihaspati; *Brahmacharini* governing the Mangal; *Shail Putra* governing the Moon; *Skanda Mata* governing the Budh; *Chandraghanta* governing the Shukra.

In her first partial expansion she devolves to Mahasaraswati. Mahasaraswati represents the Sattva Guna and is the Shakti (consort) of Brahmadev. She is the goddess of wisdom, creation and learning. She is the source of all of the arts. It is she who slew Sumbha and Nishumbha, who are symbols of ignorance. She was created from the body of Mother Parvati and is the embodiment of her hard work, spirituality and devotion. She wears yellow clothes when she takes form. When she is without form, she becomes the Primordial Sound.

The second partial expansion of Adi Parashakti embodies Mahalakshmi. She is the goddess of the material world and its preservation. She also brings good fortune and spiritual satisfaction. She is the Shakti (consort) of Narayana and is the bestower of all wealth and pleasure. She wears red Cloth. She is created from the mind of Mother Parvati. Mother Mahalakshmi is the primary deity of the Raja Guna. When she is formless, she becomes light.

Mahakali is the third partial expansionary form of Adi Parashakti. She fulfills the spiritual thirst of the mankind and presides over the destruction of the universe as well. She gives salvation (moksha) to mankind. She is the Shakti and consort of Shiva. She helped Vishnu slay the demons Madhu and Kaitabha. Parvati is same as Yogmaya also known as Tamsi Devi as per Durga Saptashati. Parvati wears blue and presides over the Tamas Guna. When she is formless, she becomes heat.

Divine Mother Adi Parashakti has been accepted as Brahman, in Hinduism ever since the time of Upanishads. Each individual deity is to be understood as a partial manifestation of Brahman, which ultimately is beyond all specifying attributes, functions, and qualities. Goddess Adi Shakti as the Brahman affirms her superior position in the Hindu pantheon. Her being the Brahman evolves two central philosophical points congenial to the theology of the Mahadevi: (a)She is ultimate reality itself, (b)The source of all divine manifestations, male and female (but especially female).

As saguna Brahman, Mahadevi or the Adi Parashakti is portrayed as a great cosmic queen enthroned in the highest heaven. Multitude of deities is her agents through which she governs the infinite universes.

Brahmadev realises that Adi Shakti divides herself to Purusha and Prakriti from single seed. Adi Parashakti incarnates in complete materialistic form as Param Prakriti from the left half of Shiva. Adi Shakti's Saguna Swaroop i.e. Parvati assumes the form of Yoni and Shiva assumes the form of Linga and their union brings evolution of life. Thus Brahmadev updates his knowledge that Parvati (incarnation of Adi Shakti) is lineal progenitor of all other goddesses (which are essentially her various forms and names). Devi Bhagwat Purana confirms this when Trimurti and demigods praises Adi Shakti:

> *"Srishti Sthiti Vinasham Shakti Bhute Sanatane*
>
> *Guna Shaye (Devoid of all attributes i.e. Nirguna)*
>
> *Gana maye (Having all the attributes) Narayani Namaustute"*

This means: We bow to the first female (Narayani), the eternal energy, who creates, sustains and destroys all the elements i.e. tattva and the one who is truly supreme spirit (Nirguna) at the time who encapsulate all the attributes for Generation, Observation and Destruction.

Ж Ψ Φ Ω ↀ

Worshipping Adi Shakti amongst Hindus is spontaneous reality. Throughout India, devotees worship Devi Adi Shakti in their temples and at wayside shrines.

The Goddess is older than time, yet time itself. She is formless, yet found in all forms. Her presence is in all things, yet she transcends all things. She is ever-changing, yet eternally changeless. She is both the womb from which all life flows forth and the tomb to which all life returns. Devi is the source of the life-giving powers of the universe. She is experienced by her ecstatic worshipers as the Primal Cause and Mother of the World.

To know the Goddess is to experience Being-Consciousness and bliss itself. This necessitates total surrender on the part of her followers before she condescends to reveal herself in her divine state. Her fervent devotees must learn to see her presence in all things. She must become the bedrock and the meaning of their life. Then, and only then, can they aspire to experience her blessings in their totality. We learn to accept the dark side of our own in our psychological evaluation. Similarly it is necessary to understand the Goddess in her terrible aspect also. While Adi Shakti is the bestower of life, as Kali the personification of all-consuming Time she is also its destroyer. To Goddess Kali at the appointed time, all manifested things return. They are absorbed into her being, there to await rebirth in yet another cycle of cosmic creation.

Practitioners of Shaktism worship the Goddess Adi Shakti in all her manifestations. Her human or *Shakti Swaroop* (*powerful form*), Parvati, was married to Shiva, while her *Gyan Swaroop* (*knowledge form*), Saraswati, weds Brahmadev and her *Dhan Swaroop* (*wealth form*), Lakshmi, becomes the consort of Vishnu.

Devi-Mahamaya Purana says,

> *"By you this universe is borne, by you this world is created,*
> *Oh Devi, by you it is protected."*

Shaktisangama Tantra says,

"Woman is the creator of the universe, the universe is her form; woman is the foundation of the world, she is the true form of the body. In woman is the form of all things, of all that lives and moves in the world. There is no jewel rarer than woman, no condition superior to that of a woman."

Adi Shankaracharya advocates in the Smarta Advaita,

"Shakti is one of five equal personal forms of God in the panchadeva system".

Mother Durga as Adi-Shakti is worshipped by all tantric sect as Nirguna and Saguna Brahman (eternal spirit, formless and with form), and shabda Brahman (eternal sound).

Followers of the Vedas worship Adi Shakti as Param-Brahman or the eternal spirit. Adi-Shakti manifests in the male forms of Brahmadev, Vishnu, and Shiva as their active force.

ЖΨΦΩↂ

Furthermore the philosophical need of the human is fulfilled by her role with cosmogony.

Since the dawn of human understanding it is known that there cannot

be any origination whatsoever without the union of the Male and Female aspects. This analogy on being extended to the universe as a whole establishes the concept of the primordial Father and Mother.

Tantrics (Shakta devotees of Devi Adi Shakti) tend to view this power as universal energy possessed by a female counterpart. Shakti being conceived as the counterpart of the possessor (in this case Shiva), came to be recognised as the consort of Shiva. This is true not only in the Shakta tradition but in almost all other traditions viz., the Shaivas (believers in Shiva as the supreme), the Suryas (believers in the Sun), the Ganapatyas (believers in Ganesha), and the Vaishnavas (believers in Vishnu).

There is seldom a god or demi-god for which a consort is not conceived as an inseparable Shakti. The "Shakti" of Indra is Sachi

(Indrani), meaning power. Indrani is part of a group of seven or eight mother goddesses called the Matrikas (Brahmani, Vaishnavi, Maheswari, Indrani, Kaumari, Varahi and Chamundi or Narasimhi), who are considered Shaktis of major Hindu gods (Brahmadev, Vishnu, Shiva, Indra, Skanda, Varaha/Yama and Narasimha respectively). Interestingly this strong belief in the Goddess Shakti has brought about a popular synthesis among philosophies like Samkhya, Vedanta, Vaishnavism, and Tantra. In the real world of humanity every wife stands as the Shakti of every husband.

Samkhya speaks of 'Purusha' and 'Prakriti' as two independent and ultimate realities. In the Puranas and other literatures Prakriti have been practically identified with the Shakti and Shiva of the Tantras. In a similar manner the principle of Maya (illusion) has been conceived as the Shakti of Brahman. These pairs were later viewed in the form of Vishnu and his Shakti, Lakshmi. Thus, in popular belief, Purusha-Prakriti of Samkhya or Shiva-Shakti of the Tantras, Brahman-Maya of Vedanta or Vishnu-Lakshmi of Vaishnavism, all mean the same.

Hindu Upanishad projects that in the beginning there have been the Cosmic Being as the Atman in human form. He has been unsatisfied. Then there rouses desire in the Atman to have companion. He thinks that he is consisting of male and female lay unified as if deeply embraced. This 'willing' of the Cosmic Being may be recognised as the first vibration of the Shakti creating the first cosmic rhythm in the absolutely calm and quiet ocean of darkness.

In this first vibration of activity, she acquires independence and tends to manifest herself in her triple functions of 'willing' (icchha), 'knowing' (jnana), and 'activity' (kriya). These three functions are symbolised by the inverted triangle, called the Yantra of the Mother Goddess.

Power of Shakti is never viewed as a separate entity from the agent that possesses the power. The awakening of Shakti therefore means the awakening of the agent from his infinitely contracted state to the state of full-fledged 'Infiniteness'. Shakti is thus the full 'Infiniteness' of the power. Her nature is infinite bliss. So He divided himself into two, male and female, which formed the first pair. All the pairs of creation are said to be the replicas of this original pair. The union of these two – energy and matter being the consumer and the consumed represents the two aspects of the one non-dual truth. One is internal, illuminating, unchangeable, and immortal while the other external, obstructive, gross and perishable.

Appearance of the Adi Parashakti has been described in our Puranas. In one of the Puranas She is described to have invited the Trimurti to her celestial abode. The Trimurti sees the goddess sitting on a jeweled seat in a chariot drawn by seven lions. Her face contains the radiance of millions of stars and her celestial beauty is so great that the Trimurti is not able to look at her. She carries trishul, shield, mace, bow, arrow, chakra, long sword and right hand as abhaya mudra. They then realise that she is the energy responsible for creating, preserving, and destroying the whole universe.

It further says, Adi Shakti is Tridevi – Kali, Lakshmi, Saraswati – the equal half and eternal beloved consort of Trimurti (the three aspects of Godhead). Divine Mother Adi Parashakti is "Divine Pure Eternal Consciousness" manifested as Shiva-Shakthi. All the gods and goddesses are her manifestations of various vibratory divine entities. As Shakti, she becomes the powerful spiritual energy without which the God is unable to act.

Her protective and maternal side of nature is manifested in the images of her priestesses, the Yoginis and Shaktas. Organic forms such as branches or vines symbolises Nature in its most instinctive form of magical medicinal power. In the form of a sacred river Saraswati she is the leader and protector of the spoken word, as well as all intellectual and artistic pursuits. In her Laxmi manifestation she is that of the beneficent Lakshmi, giver of prosperity and abundance.

Adi Shakti is revered as the pre-Vedic Virgin Bride. Devi Sati epitomises the loyal and virtuous wife who is faithful to her husband even unto death. Devotees believe her Motherly presence within all her creations. She is their Mother. She gives them life. She nurtures them through and remain present in their times of need. Through her worship, devotees can transcend the world of illusion and reach out to her true being.

After a long period Brahmadev wakes up and comes out of his deep thoughts. He feels enriched with his comprehension on Adi Shakti.

Ж Ψ Φ Ω ↂ

Chapter 3

Creation Accelerates

Essential need of the moment has driven Operator for a thorough introspection with the truth about Adi Shakti.

The self-introspection has now been over.

Comprehending much about Adi Shakti, Operator decides to excogitate Shiva, the Supreme ascetic knowledge provider.

Operator engages in worshipping Ardhnaarishwar form of Shiva. Shiva becomes pleased with his austerity and appears in the form of Ardhnaarishwar that is half male and half female. The half male part is known to be the Shiva and half female part is known to be Adi Shakti.

Pleased with his act Shiva asks Brahmadev for a boon.

Operator requests Shiva to separate Shakti from him (Shiva) as he needs the energy (Shakti) to create the living world.

Shiva agrees.

Thus, Shakti stands separated from Shiva.

The Separated Shakti is nature and hence also known as Prakriti.

Goddess Adi-Shakti emerges, separating from Shiva. Goddess promises to help Brahmadev whenever required in the creation of the world.

Shiva gives away his consort Adi-Shakti to the world for its welfare through Brahmadev's creation. Shiva is left without Shakti. He will now be concentrating fully on meditation. He will be away to his world of Yoga for seeking replies to many questions of the universe.

Operator returns to Brahmaloka and spends many years completely alone and isolated. Isolation provokes him to undertake the act of creation of living being in the world.

His understanding is completed after he encounters the Ardhnaarishwar form of Shiva. This form of Shiva highlights the fact that Purusha or Male form drawing aesthetic energy of Shiva combines with the 'Female' or 'Ishtri' form drawing aesthetic energy of Adi Shakti to create the united form of Shiva where Adi Shakti as his soul mate existed as half female in his body.

After Brahmadev revives his posture and put his senses and acts together, he becomes creator. The manifested world of plurality emerges from the unmanifested Reality. In the endeavour Brahmadev is endowed with Saraswati (one form of Adi Shakti) as his consort and consciousness at the time of creation. She is considered to be "the embodiment of his power, the instrument of creation and the energy that drives his actions".

Maitri Upanishad asserts that the universe emerges from darkness (Tamas), first as passion (Rajas), which then refines into purity and goodness (Sattva). Of these three qualities, Rajas is mapped to Brahmadev. Subsequent epics, conflate Brahmadev with Purusha. Hindu theory of cosmogony in the Puranas suggests Brahmadev as the "secondary creator" as he is associated with the continuous creation, evolution, dissolution and then re-creation in an endless repeating cycle of existence.

Brahmadev and Saraswati together form the base. All knowledge, religious and secular emanate from them. Through her exceptional knowledge she bore Brahmadev the four *Vedas* (holy books of Hinduism), all branches of knowledge, the 36 Raginis and 6 Ragas of music, ideas such as Memory and Victory, Yoga, religious acts, speech, Sanskrit, and the various units of measurement and time

The thoughts and the consciousness support from his consort induce in him the realisation that creation of living being can be achieved by creating the creatures who can be engaged by copulative processes.

The aspects of creation of living beings come up with the beginning of the Swayambhava Manvantara. From Brahmadev, continuing to meditate, are born mind-engendered progeny, with forms and faculties derived from his corporeal nature; embodied spirits, produced from the person of that all-wise deity. These beings are called the mind-born sons (Manas Putra) of Brahmadev. The state of their consciousness is summarized as the Seer with the same understanding of Brahmadev. Brahmadev in turn, can confer this state of consciousness upon others who prove themselves capable and worthy.

Ж Ψ Φ Ω ☪

In his initial effort to create Manasputra, the first four named Sanaka, Sanatana, Sanandana and Sanatkumara refuses to assist Brahmadev in his creation process and proceed to be in Bramhacharya forever.

The process of creation continues.

In the next action Brahmadev separates himself into two parts, the male and the female after dividing the golden egg. Male springs from him named Viraj and the female named Shatarupa, a beautiful woman. From Viraj springs Manu. Humans are descended from Manu and came to be known as Manava.

Manu marries Shatarupa and produce three sons named Vira, Priyavrata and Uttanapada. Uttanapada's son is the Dhruva. Dhruva performs very severe penance (Tapasya) for three thousand years. Pleased Brahmadev grants Dhruva an eternal place in the sky and comes to know as the pole star.

Brahmadev creates good & evil, light & dark from his own person. He creates the four types: gods, demons, ancestors and human.

Brahmadev then makes all living creatures on the earth. Myths wraps around many of these creations. One of them goes as follows: After the creation of first woman Shatarupa, Brahmadev becomes infatuated with her due to her beautiful look and chased her. But the woman feels Brahmadev's desire not appropriate as he himself has created her. So she eludes him and takes many shapes of animals. First she takes the form of cow when Brahmadev takes the form of bull. Together they create cows. Like that they together give birth to a series of animals.

In the initial process of creation, in a moment of distraction, the demons are born from Brahmadev's thigh. So he abandons his own body and the Night follows. After Brahmadev creates good gods he abandons his body once again, which then become Day. Hence demons gain the ascendancy at night and gods, the forces of goodness, rule the day. Brahmadev then creates ancestors and men, each time again abandoning his body so that they become Dusk and Dawn respectively. This process of creation repeats itself in every Aeon or Kalpa.

Here comes the period of Swayambhava Manvantara.

Brahmadev continues his creations. He once again engages in making mind-born sons. He successfully creates 10 more Manas putras. They are Marichi, Atri, Pulaha, Pulastya, Angiras, Kratu, Vashishtha, Narada, Daksha and Bhrigu. Of these ten Manas-putra first seven become famous Sages and Rishis. They form what we know as the Sapta-Rishi constellation. These seven along with Bhrigu and Daksha carry out initially the process of Srishti. They are considered as primary ancestral origins of the human race. Narada does not participate in the creation process and remains as a bachelor to undertake the job of messenger between Gods and men.

Brahmadev further creates two more of his manas-putra Kardama and Dharma.

Brahmadev has been a great dreamer.

After the creation of the early set of mind-sons Brahmadev become more restless.

A beautiful lady springs from Brahmadev's mind.

On seeing her, Daksha along with his 9 brothers and Brahmadev himself all get charged up with lust.

Various thoughts run through the males thus roused.

At this time from Brahmadev, Kama, the god of love is born.

Brahmadev then asks Daksha to get a suitable wife for Kama.

After Brahmadev finishes his creation, Kama decides to test his powers.

Kama by his power then makes Brahmadev, Daksha, and his other seven brothers attracted to Sandhya, a sibling of Kama and the epitome of chastity.

Daksha is overcome by lust.

Dharma is the most ascetic among Brahmadev's manas putras. Seeing the unethical behaviour of his brothers he prays to Shiva. He tells them that what they are doing is wrong.

Out of embarrassment for his actions, excited Daksha starts sweating. Out of this sweat, Rati is born.

After Brahmadev and Shiva disappear, King Daksha gets his daughter Rati married to Kama. Marriage is held with all pompous.

After the marriage, everyone goes back to their respective abodes.

ЖΨΦΩↀ

Chapter 4

Operator Makes Blunders

In human perception His look has given rise to many controversies.

Arriving at an iconic form for Brahmadev is embedded in a mystery.

At the beginning of the creation, when Brahmadev separates himself in to two – a male and a female, the female creation comes out to be very beautiful.

Infatuated Brahmadev cannot take away his eyes from her. So he turns to the direction wherever she goes. In the process he develops five heads.

So originally Brahmadev used to have five heads. This is very symbolic in terms of conveying favourably about the evolution.

Amongst many intrigued Hindu myths associated with the look of Brahmadev one legend has gone into as follows:

With many years of creation process going on, a large numbers of demons are created.

In due course some of the disgruntled and jealous demons get united. They attack the abodes gods and goddesses to dethrone them and occupy their abodes.

A terrible war takes place between the Gods and the Demons. In the said war the Gods lose and are stood dethroned.

Helpless Gods approach to Brahmadev for advice.

Brahmadev used to have five heads at that time. Brahmadev advise them to pray to Shiva.

All the Gods then approach Shiva and pray to him for helps.

Shiva appears before the helpless and demoralised Gods.

Gods say in their prayer to him – "Oh Lord!, demons have defeated us. Please kill the Demons and save us."

Hearing this Shiva assures them that he will fight with the demons.

He goes to the battle field where the demons have been harassing and torturing the Gods. With his mighty powers he attacks the demons. After a long ferocious fight he drives them off the Mount Sumeru and out of Heaven. He pursues them to the ends of the earth so that they never come back.

These entire exertions cause Shiva to sweat. Wherever the drops of sweat fall down on the ground, terrible ogresses named matris are created. These matris then start to kill the Demons and pursue them down to the underworld.

While the matris have been killing the Demons in the underworld, the surviving demons get scattered and run away.

At that time the fifth head of Brahmadev which is in the form of a donkey's head addresses the fleeing demons – "Why are you running away? Come back and fight with the Gods. I shall aid you in your fight."

Such utterances from the fifth head of Brahmadev alarm the Gods. They get surprised and confused.

This becomes a paradoxical situation.

Brahmadev is helping Gods in their flight with the Demons. But Brahmadev's fifth head tries to help the Demons.

Alarmed Gods approach to Vishnu. They inform him about all that had happened.

Then they request to him – "Oh Lord ! Please cut off Brahmadev's fifth head. It is embarrassing and causing too much of confusion".

"I can do what you want," replies Vishnu.

"But there will be a problem" Vishnu adds.

"When the cut-off head falls on earth, it will destroy the earth" Vishnu warns.

"I think you all should pray to Shiva to find a way out" Vishnu further advises them.

The gods come back to Shiva.

Once again they start praying to him.

Shiva agrees to cut off Brahmadev's fifth head. But Shiva says – "here is a problem with the disposal of the severed head. The earth and the ocean will not bear the severed head of Brahmadev".

Gods become worried again.

Finally at the wish of Vishnu, Shiva severs Brahmadev's fifth head and places it on his own matted head.

Brahmadev become sad and ashamed too.

For the first time his self-respect takes a jolt. This incidence remains as one of Brahmadev's blunders. Remembering the incidence keeps the embarrassment alive in his heart.

Since then Brahmadev got the iconographic description having four-faced head each face points to a cardinal direction.

ЖΨΦΩↀ

Hindus associate these four faces with the creation of four Vedas (Rig, Yajur, Sama, and Atharva), four Yugas of time (Krita or Satya, Treta, Dwapara, Kalki), and four Varnas (Brahman, Kshatriya, Vaisya, Sudra). Architecture of the temples dedicated to Brahmadev show his Vishwakarma aspect with four heads.

His appearance has mystic symbolism too like other deities in Hinduism. The lotus represents the Reality. Brahmadev sitting on the lotus indicates that he is ever-rooted in the infinite Reality. Reality is the foundation on which his personality rests. The four faces also symbolize the functioning of the inner personality (antahkarana) which consists of thoughts. They are the mind (manas), the intellect (buddhi), ego (ahamkara) and conditioned-consciousness (chitta). They represent the four ways in which thoughts function. They are the manifestations of the unmanifested consciousness.

Mystery of the Satyaloka consisting of the cosmology, the creation, the philosophy, art and life, is centered on Brahmadev and goddess Saraswati. It is keenly associated with his actions and the consequences thereof.

Innovative creations perhaps tend to set in arrogance in Brahmadev resulting some of his weakest moments in his tenure of first Kalpa.

That has been the occasion when Brahmadev and Vishnu involve in an argument about who of them is superior to the other. Both tries to justify their positions but the arguments and counter arguments keep on continuing without any resolution.

Right then, amidst their heated discussion, an inexplicable blazing pillar of light appears in front of them, whose root and tip are not visible.

The roots of the light pillar seem to have penetrated deep into the earth with the tip piercing into the skies beyond eternity.

Both the Gods got amazed by the view of this pillar of bright light.

They were awe struck by the brilliance of the light beam. They wondered about this third entity that stood there challenging both of their supremacy.

Their arguments get subdued and take a pause.

They ponder over the situation and start to think how to deal with that new entity.

All on a sudden, there hears a divine oracle out of nowhere,

This asks them to compete with one another to find the start and end of the blazing pillar. One who can reach the targeted spot first will be the winner of the competition.

Following the divine oracle both Brahmadev and Vishnu set out to locate the start and end of that pillar.

Brahmadev turns himself into a goose and fly upwards to find the top of the pillar. Vishnu transforms himself into a boar and start digging deep into the earth to find the end of the pillar.

Both try tirelessly. The search goes on for ages but the outcome proves futile as neither of them succeed in their respective missions.

After their unsuccessful attempts, both Brahmadev and Vishnu feel humbled.

They come back to their original place only to find Shiva manifesting in front of them.

That make them realized that there is another ultimate power already existing and rule this universe and that is Shiva. They understand that Shiva's power and cosmic existence is much beyond their imagination. They in fact realise, it is Shiva who is more powerful than both of them.

The eternity of the pillar actually symbolized the never-ending eternity of God Shiva. The fiery column of energy is the form of appearance of Shiva on the earth.

Vishnu acknowledges promptly that he could not find the lower end of the beam.

However Brahmadev lies. He says that he could find the beginning of the beam.

Brahmadev's speaking a lie annoys Shiva. Shiva curses him that he shall never be worshipped in any temple by the human being.

That is another time Brahmadev faces a huge embarrassment. His self-respect takes a bite. Insult makes Brahmadev sad and unhappy once again.

These blunders keep Brahmadev concerned for many years.

Brahmadev's mysterious mind and acts result many divine events in the ensuing time.

Chapter 5

Impatience Drives Operator

For long period Brahmadev continues his new creations. Adequate creations are put in place.

At this juncture Brahmadev's mind gets disoriented and restless.

He has been sitting in his abode at Satyaloka, remembering about the incidence that happened earlier by the presence of a female amongst them.

The embarrassing incidence does awaken him. Consequently an idea strikes his mind.

His previous encounters with Shiva were not pleasant. They have been the reason of his embarrassments.

He suddenly remembers all these which are making his mind restless. But he does not allow his desire to surface on his face.

Deep desire however allows him to feel it is the right time to give Goddess Adi-Shakti back to Shiva.

Underlying desire of Brahmadev is that Goddess Adi Shakti is brought into this world with the motive of getting her married to Shiva.

In his mind there store outlines of a long drawn plan for handling Shiva from here onwards.

He arrives at the palace of his son Daksha where all his other eight brothers are called to be present. He has also called Rati and Kama to be there.

In their presence Brahmadev says, "Shiva is a Yogi, so he despised us being attracted to a woman. If he doesn't allow men to be attracted to women, then the creation won't progress."

He pauses for a while.

All the sons keenly look at their father.

Brahmadev says, "We should get Shiva a wife".

Saying this he looks at Kama and Rati. He says "only you two are capable of accomplishing this feat".

Brahmadev advices Kama, "you and your wife shall pursue Shiva wherever he travels and seduce him."

According to Brahmadev's desire Kama and Rati tries multiple times to seduce Shiva to marry but failed every occasion.

After their failure finally Brahmadev takes this responsibility on his own shoulder.

Brahmadev becomes adamant.

In a significant move he himself decides to worship to the Goddess Adi Shakti, the Supreme Being.

Brahmadev engages in a long penance and prays to the Goddess Adi-Shakti.

Goddess Adi Shakti becomes pleased with Brahmadev's penance and appears before him.

Adi Shakti asks – "Oh Brahmadev! What do you want?"

Brahmadev prays to the Goddess, "I wish you to incarnate as the daughter of Daksha and also marry Shiva."

Goddess Adi Shakti agrees for her human incarnation and disappears.

Brahmadev becomes happy.

His plan takes off successfully as per his wish.

Happy Brahmadev then decides to meet Daksha and his wife Prasuti, the daughter of Swayambhava Manu at their palace.

He wants to convey to them the promise of Adi Shakti.

This Divine incidence rolls out a red carpet on which Brahmadev walks down with his mysterious plan.

Wonderful surrounding of Satyaloka becomes more mysterious.

Chapter 6

Kanakhala is Gifted with Divinity

It is the beginning of the Swayambhava Manvantara, first of the fourteen Manvantara in the first Kalpa (known as Pitri Kalpa).

A Manvantara is a period constituted of 306720000 human years and 14 Manvantara constitute a Kalpa, the Day time of Brahmadev. But there are periods before the first Manvantara and after the last Manvantara and in between two Manvantara, which are called Sandhikala, each of which is formed of 1728000 human years. A Sandhikala is essentially a transitional period during which the Earth is submerged in the Garbodhaka Ocean. All 14 Kalpas and 15 Sandhikalas together constitute one Day time period of Brahmadev and comprise 4320000000 human years.

One of Brahmadev's ten mind-born sons, Daksha's first birth happens during the period. He has been a man with a stocky body and a handsome face and is said to be expert in begetting children. He has been one of the Prajapatis, progenitors, agents of creation, as well as a divine King – Rishi and is associated with priestly skills.

In due course Daksha becomes a powerful King. He marshals a large kingdom under his command.

One of his palaces is situated at Kanakhala from where he used to operate for discharging his obligations as Prajapati.

In due course Brahmadev gets Daksha married to Prasuti, third daughter of Swayambhava Manu and Shatarupa.

Daksha and Prasuti give birth to 22 daughters.

Swayambhava Manu is also the Mind-born son of Brahmadev.

As per the Manusmriti Svayambhuva Manu is the first Manu appears in the first Manvantara of the first Kalpa of Brahmadev.

On the other side Brahmadev has just been blessed with the promise by the Goddess Adi Shakti that she will take birth as the daughter of Daksha.

So without delay Brahmadev arrives at Daksha's palace at Kanakhala.

Daksha and his wife Prasuti welcome Brahmadev.

After settling down there Brahmadev informs them with great enthusiasm, "Goddess Adi Shakti has agreed to incarnate as your daughter".

King Daksha hears this.

But Brahmadev's enthusiasm does not percolate through Daksha's mind. His indifferent attitude prevails as he is scantly informed about Adi Shakti.

Daksha also appears a bit jittery as he is the staunch devotee of Vishnu.

Brahmadev notices both Daksha and Prasuti seem not very encouraged.

Seeing them in doubts Brahmadev updates both about Adi Shakti and advises them to go to do penance and pray to Adi Shakti for seeking her approval.

For hundreds of years, Daksha and Prasuti performed a rigorous penance, worshiping the Goddess. They give up their royal robes, put on the guises of saints and travel deep into the forest. They locate a suitable spot absolutely abandoned from the materialistic world. They sit under a big tree and start meditating on the deity. They brave harsh weather conditions and quietly remain engaged in meditation, not minding even the wild animals in the forest.

After testing them for a long time, Goddess Adi-Parashakti appears before Daksha and Prasuti and awakens them from their penance.

She appears in an effulgent form with thousand hands, holding infinite weapons. She is draped in a blood red sari and is bedecked in ornaments carved intricately, studded with gems; wearing a gold armour, a crown.

Devi is pleased with the couple's devotion.

"What boon do you want" – She asks Daksha and Prasuti

"No one is competent enough to enthrall Shiva except for you" Daksha pleads.

Continuing his prayer before Goddess he wishes "Please take birth on the Earth as our daughter and marry Shiva".

Further he says "This is the only boon I wish of you. It fulfills the interests of everyone. I have been instructed by father Brahmadev to ask for this".

"Dear Daksha, I will surely take birth in your wife's womb and marry Shiva.

But there is one condition. If ever, in the future, you are to disrespect me, I will cast off this body and take birth somewhere else," the Goddess warns and vanishes.

Daksha and Prasuti agree to take care of their "would be off-spring" and return to hermitage happily.

They are happy because the Goddess Adi Shakti is going to take birth as their daughter. However Devi's uttered condition continues to ring in the ears of Prasuti for some more time.

Ж Ψ Φ Ω ↀ

Back in their palace Daksha and Prasuti remain awaited for the Goddess Adi-Shakti to take her human birth as per the bidding of the Brahmadev.

Few years pass by.

Even after giving birth of 22 daughters, Daksha and Prasuti does not have the Goddess incarnated yet as one of their daughters.

They become worried and engaged in meditation once again.

Soon enough Prasuti becomes pregnant with a daughter who is the incarnation of the Goddess Adi Shakti. After 10 months of pregnancy, a daughter is born to Prasuti and Daksha.

Everybody rejoices. There creates a wonderful atmosphere on the Earth. Gods shower flowers on the newborn. Daksha and Prasuti name their beautiful daughter as Sati (meaning 'virtuous' woman).

The gods and sages come to the festivities and praise Sati, Daksha, and Prasuti. Many people play musical instruments. It becomes a time of joy and merriment in the palace at Kanakhala.

Kanakhala gets a Divine gift.

Holy place Kanakhala prepares for a future which Daksha Prajapati remains unaware.

ЖΨΦΩↂ

Chapter 7

New Bride Arrives at Kailash

Sati is born as the twenty third and youngest daughter of Prajapati Daksha and Prasuti. As the daughter of Daksha, Sati is also called as Dakshayani.

Daksha is the son of Brahmadev and is a great king and magnate in his own right. With his royal life style of living he renders his spiritual and philosophical guidance to mankind.

Childhood of Dakshayani is spent in the royal environment at her father's palace. She being the youngest becomes very dear to her parents.

Incidentally in bidding of Adi-Parashakti to take human birth (in this case as Sati), Brahmadev's design is that she will please Shiva with humble devotions and wed him.

It is natural that Sati even as a child adored the tales and legends associated with Shiva as narrated by sage Narada.

Her inquisitiveness about Shiva increases day by day. She grows up an ardent devotee of Shiva.

Sati is granddaughter of Brahmadev by Daksha, but is also great granddaughter of Brahmadev because Prasuti is daughter of Manu, the son of Brahmadev.

As she turns to womanhood in due course her father Daksha engages himself in the search of a suitable groom for her.

As teen Sati turns to woman she receives revelation that Shiva is the Supreme God.

She has fallen in love with him. Therefore the idea of marrying anyone else, as intended by her father, is considered by Sati as unfair.

Disturbed Sati decides on her free will to go to do penance to appease Shiva for marrying her.

In order to win over the ascetic Shiva, Sati leaves the comforts of the Royal palace.

She bid goodbye to her parents and walks into the forest.

She gives up herself to severe austerities and the constant worship of Shiva.

Going deeper into meditation, she starts by renouncing food and water. At one point of time, she would eat just one Bel leaf per day.

Then she gives up even that.

Her mother visits her in the forest and tries to coax her to eat. But she refuses to touch a morsel.

She also decides to do away with her clothing. She braves the harsh cold and lashing rains in this condition, continuing to meditate only on her . This abstinence earns her the name Aparna.

Her penance finally sees the first light of the day.

Seeing Sati's penance, Brahmadev, Vishnu, the Devas and the sages goes to Shiva and convince him to marry Sati.

Realizing the extent of her devotion to him, Shiva decides to manifest in front of her to check her resolve. After testing her resolve, Shiva finally accedes to her wishes and agrees to make her his bride.

Her penance has finally bore fruit. Sati is happy beyond belief that she has won the heart of beloved Shiva.

She then returns to her palace and waits for the D-day to arrive when Shiva would come and takes her away with him as his bride.

Shiva next calls on Brahmadev and tells him what has happened. Hearing this Brahmadev feels a sigh of relief as his plan is on the right track. He considers that the initial goal of his plan has hit the bull's eye.

An ecstatic Sati feels truly satisfied and her dream stands fulfilled. Her long drawn tapasya has met success and brought the desired result. She has own the heart of her childhood idol and guide.

ЖΨΦΩↀ

She awaits the arrival of her bridegroom, but finds her father less than elated by the turn of events.

Hearing from Shiva of his approval of marriage with Sati, Brahmadev feels confident that he has won the first step of the race against time.

Brahmadev moves ahead with his plan and meet Daksha.

In a conciliatory tone he tells Daksha "Your daughter has propitiated Shiva, who has granted her the boon."

Brahmadev further adds "Shiva is in love with Sati and cannot even focus on his meditation anymore.

I will bring Shiva here for the marriage," Brahmadev says.

Daksha dislikes Shiva and possesses extreme hatred for him.

He is never willing to hand over her favourite daughter's hand to Shiva. So Daksha remains unresponsive to Brahmadev's suggestion.

There is lot of resistance from Daksha which ultimately required the interference of Brahmadev and Vishnu.

Daksha cannot disagree and go against their wishes.

After exchange of lot of arguments and counter arguments, Daksha finally agrees to the marriage proposal brought by his father Brahmadev duly pursued by Vishnu.

Daksha starts for the wedding preparations.

Brahmadev then goes back to Shiva and informs him that Daksha has agreed to the marriage.

Shiva feels satisfied.

He knows that Goddess Shakti herself has born as Sati. Getting blessed with Sati as his consort would complete his cosmic energy.

Sati's arrogant father Daksha on the other side is far less than pleased by this turn of events.

He is a staunch Vaishnavite (devotee of Vishnu).

He cannot bear the fact that his favourite daughter is to wed someone like Shiva who is lowly placed according to him.

In any case, Sati remains firm on her decision to marry Shiva.

On the D-day Shiva got ready to go to Daksha's palace.

Accompanied by Brahmadev and all his Manas putras, Vishnu, the Devas and the sages, Shiva reaches the Royal palace of Daksha.

Shiva and his entourage are welcomed by Daksha and his citizens.

Then Daksha requests Brahmadev to perform the marriage rites.

Despite Daksha's disapproval Sati's swayamvara (a ceremony in which a bride can choose her own husband) is held when She chooses Shiva.

Daksha feels powerless to stop the wedding process.

But as is to happen it happens.

There is a major conflict crops up between Shiva & Brahmadev.

By the interference of the wisdom of the learned Sages and Rishis present there can be amicably settled.

The marriage rites get completed. Prajapati Daksha gives his daughter's hand to Shiva.

The wedding goes of peacefully in due course.

After that Daksha gives various gifts to Shiva as dowry which Shiva refuses to accept.

After the marriage is over, Shiva and Sati sit on Nandi and leaves for Mount Kailash.

Soon, Shiva and Sati reaches Kailash. Sati makes her home with Shiva in Kailash.

Sati's life with Shiva starts in the beautiful Kailash Mountain.

The unique snow clad mountainous surroundings are partly religious where great Sages and Rishis are engaged in daily rituals.

Part of the green environment is like home of nomads surrounded by the Bhutas, Ganas, tribals, Tantrics, etc.

This life is quite different from the life that she had at her parent's place. Royal services are missing here. No beauty parlays, no entertainments exist here.

Of course she is aware of this life with Shiva well in advance.

Their conjugal life takes off happily.

Sati loves Shiva and Shiva loves her too. Together they spend time exclusively in beautiful mountainous environment spreading from west to east.

She has won him as her husband by undergoing severe austerities (tapas). Sati is the goddess of marital felicity and longevity in Hinduism. Sati and Shiva has nice time together in Kailash.

A human incarnation of Adi Parashakti, Dakshayani is the first consort of Shiva. She is expected to play the role of bringing Shiva away from ascetic isolation into creative participation with the household world.

While Sati enjoys her marital bliss, she has been gradually reinventing herself through meditation and yoga in the company of her husband. Shiva teaches Sati about the acts through yoga enabling her reinventing the power of Adi Shakti that she possesses.

Sati exposes herself to meditation and yoga regularly and learns her ability. She progresses slowly in reinventing herself and simultaneously remains engrossed in marital bliss and happiness with Shiva.

ЖΨΦΩ☮

Chapter 8

Vile Hatreds Vitiate the Air

Autumn mornings on the earth are very pleasant.

Sati is sitting in the midst of the tranquil environment of Kailash. Her favourite pets are in her company. She is feeding them with her own hands.

She is happily married to Shiva. Their conjugal life in Kailash is passing on peacefully.

Daksha rules over the world and its subjects, hence Daksha is known as Prajapati.

Sitting at Brahmaloka Brahmadev plans his next move.

He chooses Prajapati Daksha to take forward his plan. It is indeed a clever move.

He knows that Daksha is a staunch devotee of Vishnu only. He has inadequate knowledge about Shiva.

Above all the most striking aspect in his favour is the fact that Prajapati Daksha never likes Shiva.

At the same time the most discomforting factor for him is that Daksha is not aware of what is going on in Brahmadev's mind.

But Daksha is aware how Shiva has embarrassed and disrespected his father Brahmadev many times in the past without knowing the true facts. That hearsay information has kept alive his grudge against Shiva.

To Daksha Shiva has been the reason for the loss of the fifth head of his father Brahmadev. Shiva has been the reason for Brahmadev not being worshipped in a temple by the Hindus. So Daksha has not been keen at all to make Shiva his son-in-law.

Even after Sati's marriage he has not left any opportunity to embarrass Shiva. All these points together with mindless arrogance often provoke Daksha to cause disrespect of Shiva.

Daksha carries this villainous attitude with him towards Shiva. Brahmadev is fully aware of Daksha's this behaviour of hatred for Shiva. He recognizes this behaviour of Daksha and uses it in his favour.

Soon Brahmadev decides to enact a trailer to testify the above.

He decides to conduct a great Yajna (sacrifice), a special sacrifice to be done by the Brahmin only. The sacrifice aims to absolve Brahma of all his sins. It's a part of regular study of Vedas for propitiation of gods, sacrifice leading to moksha or salvation and practiced by all.

In this Yajna all the leaders of the universe, all the great sages, philosophers, demigods and fire-gods assemble with their followers. All the Prajapatis, gods and kings of the world are also invited. Newly married couple Shiva and Sati is also called on to participate in the Yajna.

ЖΨΦΩↀ

On the day all arrive at the Yajna place and take their seats in the ceremonial place. Daksha, the leader of the Prajapati arrives at the last.

As Daksha enters the assembly hall his bodily lustre is seen as bright as the effulgence of the sun and the entire assembly gets illuminated. Influenced by his great personality all the fire-gods and other participants with the exceptions of Brahmadev and Shiva stand up in respect for Daksha.

Daksha is adequately welcomed by the presiding priest Brahmadev.

After reciprocating admiration and reverence to father Brahmadev he takes his seat.

Before taking his seat, Daksha however notices that Shiva continues to sit and not showing him any respect.

Prajapati Daksha feels offended seeing Shiva sitting.

Brahmadev being Daksha's father and Shiva being Daksha's son-in-law are considered superior in stature to Daksha.

But proud Daksha misunderstands Shiva's gesture. He takes Shiva's gesture as an insult. Daksha vows within himself to take revenge on the insult in the same manner.

Daksha becomes very angry. Anger driven Daksha with his eyes glowing cannot resist him-self anymore.

He stands up and begins to speak very strongly against Shiva.

He addresses the gatherings in his familiar voice filled with pride and arrogance saying "All sages, Brahmanas and Fire-gods present please hear me with attention for I speak about the manners of gentle persons. I do not speak out of ignorance or envy".

He continues "Shiva has spoiled the name and fame of the governors of the universe. He has polluted the path of gentle manners. Because he is shameless, he does not know how to act".

Continuing further he says "Shiva has already accepted himself as my subordinate by marrying my daughter in the presence of fire and Brahmanas. He has married my daughter, who is equal to Gayatri and has pretended to be just like an honest person".

Daksha continues speaking, "Shiva has eyes like monkeys, yet he has married my daughter, whose eyes are just like those of a deer cub. Nevertheless he does not stand up to receive me, nor does he think it fit to welcome me with sweet words. I have no desire to give my daughter to this person, who has broken all rules of civility.

Because of not observing the required rules and regulations, he is impure, but I am obliged to hand over my daughter to him just as one teaches the messages of the Vedas to a Sudra."

Brahmadev and Vishnu hear all these but maintained calculated silence.

Daksha then resorted to mudslinging by attacking Shiva's personal lifestyle.

He speaks loudly – "Shiva lives in filthy places like crematoriums, and his companions are the ghosts and demons. Naked like a madman, sometimes laughing and sometimes crying, he smears crematorium ashes all over his body. He does not bathe regularly, and he ornaments his body with a garland of skulls and bones.

Therefore only in namesake is he Shiva, or auspicious; actually, he is the most mad and inauspicious creature. Thus he is very dear to crazy beings in the gross mode of ignorance, and he is their leader".

Adding further Daksha says – "On the request of Brahmadev I handed over my chaste daughter to him, although he is devoid of all cleanliness and his heart is filled with nasty things."

Seeing Shiva still sitting, Daksha stops speaking, washes his hands and mouth.

He then curses Shiva in the following words "The demigods are eligible to share in the oblations of sacrifice, but Shiva, who is the lowest of all the demigods, should not have a share".

All members of the sacrificial assembly stand up and in a united voice protest this statement of Daksha.

Daksha remains undeterred and completes cursing Shiva and then leaves the assembly in a hurry. He goes back to his home.

ЖΨΦΩↀ

Nandiswara one of Shiva's principal associates has been listening to Daksha's uttering. He realises that his master Shiva has been cursed.

He has great anger. His eyes become red.

He prepares to curse Dakṣa and all the Brahmanas present there who have tolerated Dakṣha's cursing Shiva.

He starts speaking in very harsh words – "Anyone who accepts Dakṣa as the most important personality and neglects Shiva because of envy is less intelligent and because of visualizing in duality will be bereft of transcendental knowledge."

Continuing his speech Nandiswara says – "Pretentiously religious householder life, in which one is attracted to material happiness and thus also attracted to the superficial explanation of the Vedas, robs one of all intelligence and attaches one to fruitive activities as all in all."

He continues his cursing Dakṣa saying "Daksha has accepted the body as all in all. Therefore since he has forgotten the Vishnu-pada or Vishnu-gati and is attached to sex life only within a short time he will have the face of a goat.

Those who have become as dull as matter by cultivating materialistic education and intelligence are necessarily involved in fruitive activities. Such men have purposely insulted Shiva."

Nandi further says – "May they continue in the cycle of repeated birth and death, May those who are envious of Shiva, being attracted by the flowery language of the enchanting Vedic promises, and who have thus become dull, always remain attached to fruitive activities.

These Brahmanas (priests) take to education, austerity and vows only for the purpose of maintaining the body. They shall be devoid of discrimination between what to eat and what not to eat. They will acquire money, begging from door to door, simply for the satisfaction of the body."

Thus Nandiswara curses all the hereditary Brahmanas.

After hearing Nandiswara all along sage Bhrigu stands up and starts to condemn the followers of Shiva.

He says with this strong Brahminical curse: "One who takes a vow to satisfy Shiva or who follows such principles will certainly become an atheist and be diverted from transcendental scriptural injunctions.

Those who vow to worship Shiva are so foolish that they imitate him by keeping long hair on their heads. When they are initiated into worship of Shiva, they prefer to live on wine, flesh and other such things".

Bhrigu Muni continues – "Oh Nandiswara! Since you blaspheme the Vedas and the Brahmanas who are followers of the Vedic principles it is understood that you have already taken shelter of the doctrine of atheism.

The Vedas give the eternal regulative principles for auspicious advancement in human civilization, which have been rigidly followed in the past. The strong evidence of this principle is the Supreme Personality of Godhead, Janardana, the well-wisher of all living entities.

By blaspheming the principles of the Vedas, which are the pure and supreme path of the saintly persons, certainly you followers of Bhutapati Shiva will descend to the standard of atheism without a doubt".

Under such on-going cursing and counter cursing Shiva becomes very morose. Not saying anything Shiva with wife Sati leave the arena of the sacrifice.

All his disciples and followers also follow him in silence.

Sati feels very sad and unhappy. Her father's hateful speech has hurt her to the core. She also realises how worst Shiva must be feeling. Feeling of detaching relationship with her father Daksha set in her mind.

Daksha's first birth life is a story of hatred for Shiva. This starts to reveal.

Chapter 9

Sadness Batters Kailash

Hindu legend depicts Daksha Prajapati a proud and arrogant king.

Hardcore devotee of Vishnu Daksha does not get on with his renunciative son-in-law Shiva.

He cannot reconcile to the fact that Shiva is his son-in-law. He hates Shiva from the corc of his heart.

He has not kept any contacts to know well-being of her daughter after marriage. For all purpose he has excommunicated his favourite daughter Sati from the rest of the family.

King Daksha has never accepted Sati's worship and devotion of Shiva.

Alternatively these practices have strengthened unmarried Sati's immense desire to become Shiva's wife.

Daksha has not liked his daughter's yearning for Shiva, mainly because he is a Prajapati and the son of the god Brahmadev. His daughter Sati is a royal princess. They are wealthy, noble and their imperial royal lifestyle is entirely different from that of Shiva.

As a King, Daksha has the inclination to increase his influence and power through marital relation with powerful empires and influential sages and scholars.

Shiva on the other hand leads a very modest life.

He lives among the downtrodden, wear a tiger skin, smears ashes on his body, has thick locks of matted hair and begs with a skull as bowl.

His abode is the Mount Kailash in the Himalayas.

He embraces all kinds of living beings and does not make any distinction between good souls and bad souls. The Bhutaganas, his followers, consist of all kinds of ghosts, demons, ghouls and goblins.

He wanders through gardens and graveyard alike.

As a consequence, Daksha always has an aversion towards Shiva being his daughter's companion.

This lead to Daksha's hatred of the ascetic Shiva grows even stronger because Shiva is now his son-in-law.

Sati marries Shiva. Daksha forbids it, but Sati disobeys him and does so anyway, finding in Shiva a doting and loving husband.

Daksha dislikes Shiva intensely, calling him a dirty, roaming ascetic and reviling the great yogi's cohort of goblins and ghouls, not knowing Shiva being the Supreme Brahman.

Daksha also has developed a grudge against Shiva by keeping alive misinformation that Shiva has caused a few embarrassments to his father Brahmadev.

Daksha's grudge towards Shiva grows further after Brahmadev's Yajna. The tension between the father-in-law and son-in-law, Daksha and Shiva, continues for a considerably long period. Daksha doesn't put the matter at rest.

ЖΨΦΩↀ

After sometime Brahmadev upgrades the status of Daksha and appoints him the chief of all the Prajapatis, the progenitors of the population. Daksha becomes very much puffed up and his arrogance knows no bound.

Boastful Daksha decides to celebrate this great occasion by organizing a great sacrificial Yajna. He named it 'Vajpayee' and arranged it in a newly built palace annexed to his palace at Kanakhala.

Kanakhala used to be a small colony near present day Haridwar. This is said to be the place where Prajapati Daksha's palace used to be located. Today we may see a temple there named Daksheswara Mahadev temple. It is believed Kanakhala used to be the summer capital of Shiva and a holy place to the sages.

Daksha become excessively confident of his support by Brahmadev in the matter. As he keeps his hatred on Shiva alive, so the underline motive of the Yajna is to insult Shiva.

Daksha initiates the great sacrifice at Kanakhala in the southern part of Haridwar in the same manner as that of Brahmadev. The Yajna is to be presided over by the sage Bhrigu.

He invites all the gods, Prajapatis and kings to attend the Yajna, but intentionally avoids inviting Shiva and Sati.

ЖΨΦΩↂ

When the sacrifice is being performed at Kanakhala, Sati is sitting with her husband Shiva at Kailash.

Then there heard the sounds of the flying chariots. It comes to her view that the heavenly denizens flying in the sky. They are conversing about the great sacrifice being performed by Prajapati Daksha.

She sees that from all directions the beautiful wives of the heavenly denizens travelling by the side of her place. Their eyes are very beautifully glittering. They are going to the sacrifice ceremony dressed in fine clothing and ornamented with earrings and necklaces with lockets.

Seeing this she approaches her husband Shiva. Sati says "Dear, your father-in-law is now executing great sacrifices".

Sati continues "all the demigods invited by him are going there."' "If you desire, we may also go" she says.

Sati then tells Shiva "I think that all my sisters must have gone to this great sacrificial ceremony with their husbands just to see their relatives".

"I also desire to decorate myself with the ornaments given to me by my father and go there with you to participate in that assembly" Sati says with all excitement, her face beaming with glory.

Like any recently wedded bride she expresses "My sisters, my mother's sisters and their husbands and other affectionate relatives must be assembled there. So if I go I shall be able to see them"

"I shall be able to see the flapping flags and the performance of the sacrifice by the great sages. For these reasons, my dear husband, I am very much anxious to go" says Sati in a softer but firm note.

Sati pauses. After awhile she restarts talking.

"This manifested cosmos is a wonderful creation of the interaction of the three material modes, or the external energy of the Supreme . This truth is fully known to you.

Yet I am but a poor woman and as you know, I am not conversant with the truth. Therefore I wish to see my birthplace once more" says Sati. Adi Shakti exasperates in her human incarnation, showing too much tilt.

"Oh! Never-born, Oh! Blue-throated one, not only my relatives but also other women dressed in nice clothes and decorated with ornaments, are going there with their husbands and friends" Sati exclaims. "Just see how their flocks of white airplanes have made the entire sky very beautiful" overwhelmed Sati continues.

Oh! Best of the demigods! How can the body and mind of a daughter remain undisturbed when the daughter hears that some festive event is taking place in her father's house?"

Then Sati speaks of her mind to Shiva.

She opens up "Even though you may be considering that I have not been invited, there is no harm if one goes to the house of one's friend, husband, spiritual master or father without invitation"

After a moment turning to a conciliatory tone of request Sati says "Oh! Immortal Shiva, please be kind towards me and fulfill my desire. You have accepted me as half of your body; therefore please show kindness towards me and accept my request".

Sati has perhaps forgotten who she is and what divine power she possesses. Her birth as human daughter of a father is superseding her original past as she is being controlled by the trait of human affections at this moment.

Ж Ψ Φ Ω ⦶

Shiva, the deliverer of the Mount Kailash having thus been addressed by his dear wife, smiles and looks at her wife.

At this moment he remembers the malicious, heart-piercing speeches delivered by Daksha before the guardians of the universal affairs at Brahmadev's Yajna sometime ago.

With his smiling face he replies.

"My dear beautiful wife, you have said that one may go to a friend's house without being invited. This is true provided such a friend does not find fault with the guest because of bodily identification and thereby become angry towards him".

He clarifies "Although the six qualities education, austerity, wealth, beauty, youth and heritage are for the highly elevated, one who is proud of possessing them becomes blind and thus he loses his good sense and cannot appreciate the glories of great personalities."

"One should not go to anyone's house, even on the consideration of his being a relative or a friend, when the host is disturbed in his mind and looks upon the guest with frowning eyebrows and angry eyes" says Shiva.

Shiva keeps talking – "If one is hurt by the arrows of an enemy, one is not as aggrieved as when cut by the unkind words of a relative, for such grief continues to rend one's heart day and night".

"My dear fair complexioned lotus eyed wife, it is clear that of the many daughters of Daksha you are the most favourite, yet you will not be honored at his house because of your being my wife. Rather, you will be sorry that you are connected with me" Shiva utters in a mild scolding voice.

Shiva further exhorts – "One who is conducted by false ego and thus always distressed, both mentally and sensually, cannot tolerate the opulence of self-realized persons.

Being unable to rise to the standard of self-realization, he envies such persons as much as demons envy the Supreme Personality of Godhead."

"My dear young wife, certainly friends and relatives offer mutual greetings by standing up, welcoming one another and offering obeisances. But those who are elevated to the transcendental platform being intelligent offer such respects to the Supersoul, who is sitting within the body, not to the person who identifies with the body" clarified Shiva.

"I am always engaged in offering obeisances to Vasudev in pure Krishna consciousness. Krishna consciousness is always pure consciousness, in which the Supreme Personality of Godhead, known as Vasudev is revealed without any covering" – Shiva explained the intricacy of respectfulness.

"Therefore you should not see your father as he and his followers are envious of me. Because of his envy, O most worshipful dear one, he has insulted me with cruel words although I am innocent.

If in spite of this instruction you decide to go, neglecting my words, the future will not be good for you.

You are most respectable and when you are insulted by your near and dear one this insult will immediately be equal to death" – Shiva warns Sati.

Shiva stopped speaking.

Uttering the last few words Shiva appeared to be stressful and sad. He can foresee what is going to happen to Sati.

But as nature wishes differently he is being guided by his excessive love for Sati at this moment. He could not prevent her from going to her father's home.

Helpless Shiva gives up but he feels worried to foresee what Kanakhala has stored for her beloved Sati.

There was calm all around in Kailash, except the noises of the falling leaves. The spell of the silence was perhaps fearsome.

Sati is engrossed in deep thoughts.

Sati feels very much anxious to see her relatives at her father's house, but at the same time she is afraid of Shiva's warning.

Her mind unsettled, she walks in and out of the room like a swing.

Sati is unhappy at being forbidden to go see her relatives at her father's house. Sati's affectionate and benevolent mind brings tears in her eyes.

With a trembling body she looks at her uncommon husband for his indifferent stance towards her.

She feels anguished by Shiva's behaviour. Sati looks at Shiva as if she is going to blast him with her vision.

Hence she prays silently within herself: 'O, may my body be destroyed soon, as this body is not able to serve Shiva'.

So she decides to go alone leaving her husband Shiva in Kailash.

It is a dark moment in her life when she cannot read the writings on the wall.

Sadness rains down and engulfs the entire Mount Kailash.

Chapter 10

Kanakhala Has a Guest

Emerging from cosmic world, Shiva has been an ascetic until he falls in love with Sati.

Now when their love is set to blossom such a one-sided step by Sati does break the rhythm of their conjugal life. Though Shiva can foresee the near future, he feels momentarily sad and unhappy. He has sounded enough warning to her beloved but of no avail.

Breathing very heavily because of anger and bereavement, Sati starts walking out of Shiva's place.

Seeing Sati leaving alone from Kailash, in no times thousands of Shiva's disciples, headed by Maniman and Mada, quickly follow her with his bull Nandi in front and accompanied by the Yakshas and Ganas.

The disciples of Shiva arranges a bull on the back of which Sati will be seated.

They give her the bird which is her pet.

They bear a lotus flower, a mirror and all such paraphernalia for her enjoyment and cover her with a great canopy.

Followed by a singing party with drums, conchshells and bugles, the entire procession is as pompous as a royal parade.

Ж Ψ Φ Ω ©

On the other side, Daksha's yajna process had already begun at Kanakhala in Haridwar. A small village in a valley of the Himalayan Mountain, it contains the most sacred place where the river Ganga descends and touches the plain for the first time. The place is known as Gangadwar and is considered very sacred and auspicious. Most of the sages used to live then at this place for undertaking their spiritual persuasion.

Daksha commenced the holy sacrifice at this very auspicious place.

All the Rishis that lived on the Earth and in other regions, all of the Gods and goddesses had already arrived and taken their seats in the sacrificing site.

Brahmadev, Vishnu, and their respective followers have taken their seats.

Daksha even has invited supernatural beings such as Nagas, Gandharvas, and Vidyadharas and all the Kings with their friends, ministers, and armies.

In that magnificent congregation only missing are Shiva & Sati, whom Daksha has deliberately not invited.

A large mansion has been built at Kanakhala for the accommodations of the invitees.

Vishnu presided over the Yajna and Brahmadev was the anchor guide for the Vedic rituals.

Great Sage Dadhichi, noticing the absence of Shiva, remarked, "Oh Daksha, why have you not called Shiva. He is crucial to any sacrifice. Go call Sati and Shiva right now."

Daksha promptly replied, "I have invited Vishnu, the preserver of the universe. I have invited Brahmadev, the creator of the universe. I have called all of you. Who else is there to call? Shiva is an evil-minded man and is unworthy."

"Your destruction is imminent, Daksha. A sacrifice without Shiva is a non-sacrifice," says Dadhichi.

He knows Daksha will not give in and agree to his advice.

So saying above sage Dadhichi leaves the sacrifice arena, which is followed by a couple of other followers of Shiva.

Many whispers are heard amongst the distinguished guests of Rishis, Sages and other great people present there.

ЖΨΦΩↀ

By now Dakshayani has reached her father's house.

She proceeds to the yajna arena where the sacrifice is being performed. There are many sacrificial animals, as well as pots made of clay, stone, gold, grass and skin, which are all requisite for the sacrifice.

She stands for a while close by the Yajna place.

She finds the great Sages, Brahmanas and demigods all have assembled there. Everyone is chanting the Vedic hymns.

Sati feels sad by the absence of her Husband Shiva, the Supreme Brahman. She thinks that her father has deprived her husband from his rightful place in this Yajna. She feels disrespected deep into her core.

When Sati with her followers reaches the arena no one has taken notice of her arrival.

No one comes forward to receive her because they are all afraid of Daksha.

No one welcomes Sati, so humiliating!

Only her mother and sisters with tears in their eyes but with glad faces take notice of her from a distance. They try to talk with her pleasingly but cautiously.

Although she is received by her sisters and mother, she does not respond to their words of reception.

She is offered a seat and presents but she does not accept anything nor does she seat, as her father has neither taken notice of her yet nor has welcome her by asking about her welfare.

Reaching close to the arena of sacrifice or Yajna, Sati notices that there are no oblations for her husband Shiva.

Sometime ago this place had witnessed a strong argument occurred between Dadhichi and Daksha on the same issue.

As per the Kurma Purana, the sacrifice hymns are first offered to the twelve Aditya gods.

Immediately Dadhichi notices that there are no sacrificial portions (Havvis) allotted to Shiva and his wife.

There are no Vedic hymns used in the Yajna addressing Shiva which are part of Vedic rituals.

At once Dadhichi warns Daksha that he should not alter the Holy Vedas for personal reasons. All the priests and sages present there support this.

Daksha replies to Dadhichi that he will not do so and insults Shiva.

Sati realises that Dadhichi has left the Yajna because of this distasteful argument.

ЖΨΦΩↀ

Chapter 11

Encounter of the Heavenly Kind

Some time has elapsed since Sati's arrival at her father's house.

Standing near the Fire Sacrifice (Yajna) arena Sati realizes that not only has her father failed to invite Shiva, but he also does not receive her either.

But just then Daksha's eyes fall on standing Sati.

On seeing her arrive at the yagna, Daksha becomes furious. He starts shouting and yelling at her, hurling insults at her and Shiva.

He makes it very clear that neither she nor her husband is ever welcome there.

Sati tries to speak with her father and placate him, relating what a wonderful husband Shiva is and how happy their marriage is. However, Daksha turns a deaf ear to all this and just keeps shouting at her and humiliating her and Shiva in front of one and all present there.

Driven by arrogance Daksha's hatred for Shiva and Sati gets blown out of proportion. His foolishness makes him a puppet in the hands of unwarranted ensuing danger.

He knowingly speaks badly about Shiva and disrespects Sati.

Sati tries to make him understood but it is of no use.

Sati becomes greatly angry so much so that she looks at her father as if she is going to burn him with her eyes.

The followers of Shiva, the ghosts, get ready to injure or kill Dakṣa, but for Sati's order they all step down.

Sati looks very angry.

When Daksha does not stop yelling, angry Sati cannot take it anymore. She warns Daksha and Prasuti and reminds them about her promise that she made before she is born to them, that she would desert them if she was insulted in any way.

Accordingly, she flees into a rage and takes the form of Goddess Adi Parashakti.

Her transformed image accompanies with radiance of bright lights shows her carrying trishul, shield, mace, bow, arrow, chakra, long sword in various hands and right hand as abhaya mudra. Daksha is aware of this image of Goddess Adi Parashakti but remains undeterred

Her family and the kings, saints, sages, Gods and Goddesses present there become frightened by her terrible form.

She introduces herself to Daksha, saying that she is the Eternal Power.

Sudden lightning and thunder threatens to destroy the Earth.

All sorts of calamities arise as Mother Earth cannot bear her strong radiance and power.

The Gods, saints, sages, Goddesses Lakshmi and Saraswati, her mother and sisters tremble in fear and respectfully salute her, who is Adi Shakti, the Mother of the Universe (Jagdamba).

Adi Shakti expresses her regrets about not keeping the promises Daksha made to her before seeking her birth as his daughter.

She condemns her father for speaking ill against Shiva in the presence of all.

Goddess says – *"Shiva is the most beloved of all living entities. He has no rival. No one is very dear to him, and no one is his enemy. No one but you could be envious of such a universal being, which is free from all enmity."*

Goddess continues to rebuke Daksha – *"Twice-born Daksha, a man like you can simply find fault in the qualities of others. Shiva however never finds any faults with others' qualities, but if someone has a little good quality, he magnifies it greatly. Unfortunately you have found fault with such a great soul. It is not wonderful for persons who have accepted the transient material body as the self to engage always in deriding great souls. Such envy on the part of materialistic persons is very good because that is the way they fall down. They are diminished by the dust of the feet of great personalities".*

Then as Sati she says – *"My dear father, you are committing the greatest offense by envying Shiva, whose very name, consisting of two syllables, Si and va pronouncing of which purifies one of all sinful activities. His order is never neglected. Shiva is always pure and no one but you envies him. You are envious of Shiva, who is the friend of all living entities within the three worlds."*

She further adds *"For the common man he fulfills all desires, and because of their engagement in thinking of his lotus feet, he also blesses higher personalities who are seeking after Brahmanda [transcendental bliss]."*

"Do you think that a more respectable personality than you Brahmadev does not know this inauspicious person who goes under the name Shiva?

Does he not know that Shiva associates with the demons in the crematorium, his locks of hair are scattered all over his body and he is garlanded with human skulls and smeared with ashes from the crematorium?" asks Sati.

Sati complements by saying – "*that in spite of all these inauspicious qualities, great personalities like Brahmadev honor him by accepting the flowers offered to his lotus feet and placing them with great respect on their heads".*

"If one hears an irresponsible person like you blaspheme the master and controller of religion, one should block his ears and go away if unable to punish him. But if one is powerful and is able to kill, then one should by force cut out the blasphemer's tongue and kill the offender. After that one should give up his own life. Therefore I shall no longer bear this unworthy body, which has been received from you, who have blasphemed Shiva."

"If someone has taken a poisonous food, the best treatment is to vomit. It is better to execute one's own occupational duty than to criticize others. Elevated transcendentalists may sometimes forgo the rules and regulations of the Vedas, since they do not need to follow them, just as the demigods travel in space whereas ordinary men travel on the surface of the earth" – suggestively uttered by Sati.

In an explanatory tone sati says – "*In the Vedas there are directions for two kinds of activities — activities for those who are attached to material enjoyment and activities for those who are materially detached. In consideration of these two kinds of activities, there are two kinds of people, who have different symptoms. If one wants to see two kinds of activities in one person that is contradictory. But both kinds of activities may be neglected by a person who is transcendentally situated."*

She further says – "*My dear father, the opulence we possess is impossible for either you or your flatterers to imagine, for persons who engage in fruitive activities by performing great sacrifices are concerned with satisfying their bodily necessities by eating foodstuff offered as a sacrifice.*

We can exhibit our opulence simply by desiring to do so. This can be achieved only by great personalities who are renounced, self-realized souls."

She exhorts her frustration on herself.

She says – "*You are an offender at the lotus feet of Shiva and unfortunately I have a body produced from yours.*

I am very much ashamed of our bodily relationship and I condemn myself because my body is contaminated by a relationship with a person who is an offender at the lotus feet of the greatest personality.

Because of our family relationship when Shiva addresses me as Dakshayani I at once become morose and my jolliness and my smile at once disappear.

I feel very much sorry that my body, which is just like a bag, has been produced by you. I shall therefore give it up".

She then curses Daksha and all the Gods, princes and Goddesses of his side to be killed by Shiva.

She condemns the process of sacrificial fruitive activities and persons associated these. She curses that it will never be completed, that Tamas will subdue its Sattvik nature.

She then declares – "*from this moment, I renounce all the mortal relationships, nothing binds me anymore.*"

Then she gives her final salutations to her husband Shiva. She salutes her mother for the last time.

Sati then prays loudly with the hope – *"I shall be reborn to a father, whom I could respect."*

So saying in the arena of sacrifice Devi Sati sits down on the ground and faces north. Dressed in saffron garments, she sanctifies herself with water and closes her eyes to absorb herself in the process of mystic yoga.

First of all she sits in the required sitting posture. Then she carries the life air upwards and places it in the position of equilibrium near the navel. Then she raises her life air, mixed with intelligence, to the heart and then gradually towards the pulmonary passage and from there to between her eyebrows.

In order to give up her body as a result of her anger towards her father she begins to meditate on the fiery air within the body. Sati concentrates all her meditation on the holy lotus feet of her husband, Shiva, who is the supreme spiritual master of the entire world. By doing so she becomes completely cleansed of all taints of sin. She quits her body in a blazing fire by meditation on the fiery elements of provocation of her yogic powers. Soon the Tatva of Shakti leaves the mortal shell and the mortal body of Devi Sati collapsed on the floor in the scorching flames.

Oppressor, arrogant and foolish Daksha thus provokes her daughter Sati to the extent that she commits self-annihilation in the yajna flame.

It's a criminal offence provoking someone causing death and calls for huge reprimands from the Supreme justice system.

Daksha has committed a punishable offence before the entire spread of the Yajna participants which include Brahmadev and Vishnu among other mighty powerful gods and sages. But these two prefers to remain as silent spectators throughout the event.

ЖΨΦΩ ↀ

Chapter 12

Disasters Break Loose

There goes a famous proverb – "In every event that happens there lies seed of ensuing events ".

With Sati's death in the Yajna place, the holy place Kanakhala has already turned to a place with bad omen. It stands as a witness to the most horrendous divine event that follows.

When Sati annihilates her body in anger there occur a tumultuous roar all over the universe. Universe readily undergoes the influence of bad omen and becomes subjected to spasm of its own through natural disasters, destructions all around, loss of lives and human pains.

The great disastrous roar reaches Kailash and makes Shiva restless.

The ganas that have accompanied Sati are infuriated and starts causing havoc in the Yajna place.

Suddenly, a celestial voice comes from the sky.

It says – "Oh Daksha, how could you not listen to the warnings of Dadhichi?

How could you disrespect Sati, the great goddess, the Supreme Being?

This sacrifice will surely be destroyed, along with you. Anyone who helps you will also be destroyed!"

A great confusion erupted when this voice echoed.

The remaining ganas quickly flee to Mount Kailash to inform Shiva.

They tell Shiva everything that has occurred at the yajna.

They then request – "Please rid us of our fear and deal with these fools."

On hearing their words, Shiva calls Maharshi Narada.

Narada then goes into the detail of the event leading to the death of Sati. Shiva becomes enraged when he hears what has happened with his beloved Sati.

It is disheartening and astonishing to Shiva to hear that Daksha, who was Prajapati, the maintainer of all living entities can be so disrespectful to his own daughter Sati.

Arrogance and hatred cause perversion of mind – exemplified.

Sati is not only chaste but is also a great soul.

She gives up her body because of her father's neglect and indifference. Daksha has done filicide.

Daksha is so foul-hearted that he is unworthy to be a Brahmana.

He earns extensive ill fame because of his offenses to his daughter, because of not having prevented her death and because of his great envy of the Supreme Personality of Godhead.

ЖΨΦΩↀ

On the sacrifice arena participants are all struck clueless with the sudden death of Dakshanayani Sati, everyone's favourite.

Sati's attendants present there ready themselves to kill Daksha with their weapons.

They come forward forcibly.

Seeing the situation and the ensuing danger, Sage Bhrigu plays a trick.

He offers oblations into the southern side of the sacrificial fire immediately. He simultaneously utters hymns from the Yajur Veda.

Suddenly thousands of demigods become manifested. All of them are powerful, having achieved strength from Soma, the moon.

These demigods attack the ghosts and Guhyakas with half-burned fuel from the Yajna fire.

Sati's attendants prefer to save themselves for future fight and disperse them in different directions and disappear.

On the other side sage Narada has reached to Shiva.

Shiva hears from him about Sati's immolation because of Prajapati Dakṣha's insult to her.

Shiva also comes to know that his soldiers have been driven away by the Rbhu demigods by Bhrigu's trick. This makes Shiva greatly angry.

Grief-stricken at the same time with the demise of her beloved wife Sati, angry Shiva presses his lips with his teeth and plucks a cluster of matted hair from his head and dashes it on the ground which blaze like electricity. This hair cluster split into two parts.

From one part a black demon like personality named Virabhadra as tall as the sky and as bright as three suns combined is born.

His look is frightful, his teeth protruding dangerously and the hairs on his head flying like burning fire. He has eight hands equipped with various weapons and his garland consisting of human heads.

From the second part is born Bhadrakali, the Supreme Goddess's violent and intense incarnation, having eighteen hands holding weapons like a discus, dagger, trident, spear, mace, scimitar, sword, vajra, conch shell, demon head, drinking vessel, goad, waterpot, cleaver, shield, bow and arrow.

The gigantic demon Virabhadra salutes Shiva with folded hands and says – "What shall I do, my Lord?"

Shiva, whose other name is Bhutanatha, directly orders – "Because you are born from my body, you are the chief of all my associates. Therefore, kill Daksha and his soldiers and wreck havoc to destroy Daksha's sacrifice."

That was the simple but bold message comes in a thundering voice.

Virabhadra is the personified anger of the Supreme Personality of Godhead. He prepares to execute the orders of Shiva.

He circumambulates Shiva to acquire himself required power to cope with any threat that would put against him.

Virabhadra carries a great trident, fearful enough to kill even death and on his legs he wears bangles which seem to roar.

Many other soldiers of Shiva follow the fierce personality in a tumultuous uproar and marches forward very aggressively.

Virabhadra and Bhadrakali are assisted by eight other Goddesses named Kali, Katyayini, Chamunda, Ishaani, Mundamardini, Bhadra, Vaishnavi and Twarita who join them.

With them join hundreds of millions of ganas and Shiva's followers and together they march to the site of the yajna.

ЖΨΦΩↀ

Meanwhile at the yajna site there appears several bad omens that indicate possible disasters.

Daksha and others witnesses these signs and appear nervous.

Vishnu realises what is in store. He tells Daksha that he has been a fool that he has insulted Shiva.

Vishnu then informs Daksha about Shiva's greatness.

But it is too late.

Inglorious Daksha prays to Vishnu and gets his assurance for protection of the Yajna.

At that time persons assembled in the sacrificial arena notice sudden darkness that is gradually engulfing the arena.

Soon they realise that it is a dust storm.

All of them were anxious and perplexed.

Conjecturing on the origin of the storm they realise that there is no wind blowing and no cows are passing.

Also it is not dust storm raised by the plunderers as the powerful King Barhi is there who would punish them.

Under the circumstances no one could envisage the origin of this dust storm blowing over there.

Participants apprehended whether it is a Pralaya and the dissolution of the planet now imminent.

Prasuti, wife of Daksha, along with the other women assembled there are all became very anxious and nervous too.

They apprehend the ensuing danger created by Daksha because of the death of innocent Sati before her sisters.

Suddenly, all the ganas arrive at the yajna. Indra and all the Devas rode on their mounts and get ready to fight.

A violent battle starts between the Devas and the ganas.

In the beginning, the Devas go on the winning spree, but soon, the situation reverses. Ganas starts defeating the Devas.

Many Devas flee back to Swarga.

Only Indra and a couple others remain.

Indra and the other Devas seeks advises from Brihaspati on what to do next. Brihaspati instead of giving any suggestion tells them about Shiva's greatness and their mistake.

Meanwhile Virabhadra with all his followers has reached the battle arena.

Realising ensuing danger soon, all the remaining Devas also flee from the arena.

The ganas then enter the sacrificial hall. There they encounter Vishnu who was ready to fight.

Virabhadra asks Vishnu why he is supporting Daksha.

Vishnu replies, "I know Daksha is unrighteous. But he is a devotee of mine and has sought my refuge, so I must protect him."

Vishnu then blows his conch.

Hearing Vishnu's conch fleeing Devas returns to fight the ganas. Another battle begins.

Indra fights Nandi, Agni fights Asman and Kubera fights Kusmandapati. Mahaloka fights with Yama and Chanda fights Nairrata. Munda battled Varuna and Bhringi attacks Vayu.

Mahakali and Kshetrapala go around sucking the blood of the enemies.

Seeing this, Vishnu activates his Sudarshan Chakra and throws it at Kshetrapala. But Kshetrapala catches it and Vishnu has to forcefully take it back.

A heroic battle then breaks out between them.

Virabhadra joins Kshetrapala in attacking Vishnu. He hits Vishnu really hard with his trident and Vishnu collapses.

But Vishnu regains quickly. He stands up and gets ready to throw his chakra at Virabhadra.

But, Vishnu's chakra suddenly stops moving. He fails to throw the chakra. Vishnu starts chanting slokas and the chakra gets freed from the stunned state.

Suddenly a voice echoes from the sky.

Voice addressing Vishnu says, "The Ganas are invincible."

Enlightened, Vishnu promptly leaves for his abode Vaikunth loka in a jiffy. Seeing this Brahmadev too follows him and leaves for Satyaloka in a hurry.

Departure of the two godheads does not augur well for the sacrifice organizers.

The sacrifice arena suddenly lose its shine and turns to a orphanage in absence of two of them.

ЖΨΦΩ ↀ

Virabhadra engaged with his oppression suddenly takes notice of the Sages standing at the arena, who did not speak a word when Sati was being abused by Daksha.

He catches hold of Dharma, Kashyapa, Arishtanemi, Angiras, Krisasva Rishi, and Sage Datta and kicks them all in their heads. Sages fell down and lay injured.

He then cuts off the noses of Saraswati and Aditi, two sisters of Sati who are just got exposed before him.

He approaches Bhrigu and throws him on the ground. Manibhadra kicks him and plucks off his moustache and beard.

Chanda shatters Pusan's teeth. Nandiswara captures the demigod Bhaga and plucks out his eyes.

Baladeva knocks out the teeth of Dantavakra, the King of Kalinga.

While at Kailash, angry Shiva becomes a madman. His hairs are scattered around. He pierces the rulers of the different directions with his trident. He laughs and dances proudly, scattering their hands like flags, as thunder scatters the clouds all over the world.

The gigantic Virabhadra bares his fearful teeth.

By the movements of his brows he scatters the luminaries all over the sky and he covers them with his strong, piercing effulgence.

Because of the misbehavior of Daksha even Brahmadev and Vishnu are not able to save themselves from the great exhibition of anger and they have to leave the Yajna site.

The followers of Shiva surround the arena of sacrifice.

They are of short stature and are equipped with various kinds of weapons. Their bodies appear to be like those of sharks, blackish and yellowish.

They run all around the sacrificial arena and begin to create disturbances. Some of the soldiers pulled down the pillars which have been supporting the pandal of sacrifice.

Some of them enter the female quarters, some begin destroying the sacrificial arena, and some enter the kitchen and the residential quarters. They break all the pots made for use in the sacrifice.

Few begin to extinguish the sacrificial fire. Some tear down the boundary line of the sacrificial arena and some pass urine on the arena.

Other group of followers of Shiva blocks the way of the fleeing sages while some threatens the women assembled there.

Some arrested the demigods who are seen fleeing the pandal.

There have been continuous showers of stones in all directions. All the priests and other members assembled at the sacrifice are put to immense misery. For fear of their lives they try to disperse in different directions.

Just then Virabhadra spots Daksha hiding behind the sacrificial altar.

He grabs Daksha by the cheeks. Virabhadra kicks him down on the floor and then sit on his chest. He tries to separate his head from his body with sharp weapons, but fails. He then tries to cut the head of Daksha with hymns as well as weapons but still it is hard to cut even the surface of the skin of Daksha's head. Virabhadra gets exceedingly bewildered. Then his eyes fall on the wooden device in the sacrificial arena by which the animals are sacrificed. With that he gets Daksha beheaded promptly.

Virabhadra and members of his team shout with ferocious laughter that tremble the entire arena. They accomplish their job.

Shiva's order stands honoured.

Upon seeing the action of Virabhadra, the party of Shiva becomes pleased.

All the bhutas, ghosts and demons shout joyously which make a tumultuous sound.

Virabhadra then takes the severed head of Daksha in his hand. With great anger he throws it into the southern side of the sacrificial fire offering it as an oblation amidst the thunderous noises of joy of Shiva's followers.

In this way devastation of all the arrangements for sacrifice stands completed by the followers of Shiva.

After setting fire to the whole arena, they depart for their master's abode Kailash.

Daksha's Yajna place ends in an inauspicious hip of ashes. Holy place Kanakhala stands as a mute witness to the mysterious divine event, which has taken a few lives.

ЖΨΦΩ

Chapter 13

The Tandava Nritya

Grief stricken Shiva reaches the fire sacrifice arena at Kanakhala. He looks at his beloved's motionless half burnt body.

Alas! Shiva can do nothing to get Sati back alive.

He remembers before ending her life at her will Sati has pronounced that she does not wish to reborn ever as daughter of Daksha and has denounced all her mortal relation with that family.

Helplessness makes Shiva appearing extremely broken down but angry at the same time.

With grief and sorrow Shiva then picks up still body of her beloved wife on his arms and starts walking.

After sometime angry Shiva puts Sati's body on his shoulder and walks like a wild crazy man.

In this manner furious Shiva starts dancing carrying his beloved's body on his shoulder, reminiscing their moments as a couple and begins to roam around the universe.

Shiva is distressed and wanders around universe in his extremely aggressive posture of his wild dance termed as the Tandav Nritya.

This dance causes whole universe to shake in the form of earthquakes. Wide scale destruction prompted thereafter causes great loss to lives and properties.

Holy place Kanakhala stands as the mute witness to the reason for Shiva's Tandav Nritya.

Seeing the imminent danger to the world and the mankind as grave as "Pralaya", all Gods become afraid and approach Vishnu.

They request Vishnu to use his power to calm down Shiva.

Vishnu justifies himself with the thoughts that as long as Shiva is mentally and physically attaches with Sati's body, his destructive dance cannot be controlled.

So to reduce grief-stricken Shiva's pain and agony Vishnu decides to detach Sati's body from Shiva.

For doing this he activates his Sudarshan Chakra. The rotating disc severs Sati's corpse into multiple parts.

As Shiva has been moving all over the universe with Sati's corpse, so severed body parts of Sati fall at different places on the earth.

These places on the earth thus become connected with Goddess Sati's life through her severed body parts which remains there eternally in the form of abode of Adi Shakti.

As Sati's body is no more there on Shiva's shoulder Shiva gradually become sober.

His Tandav Nritya stops. The universe stands saved.

Without Sati grief stricken Shiva goes in isolation, solitude ages, wanders around for quite sometimes before finally settles down at Kailash.

Vishnu has done right in detaching Sati's corpse from Shiva by disintegrating her body in to multiple pieces.

But he has failed to assess at that moment that his action has become the reason for consolidating the ground of the Shakti worshippers and the Shakta sects consequently.

Vishnu thus unknowingly sowed the great seed for promotion of Shaktism.

Brahmadev on the other hand feels happy within himself.

He succeeds in taking revenge that Shiva stands hurt hard at his weakest point. Goddess Adi Shakti will no more be part of his being.

Simultaneously he feels sad that Daksha has to lose his life in the process.

Ж Ψ Φ Ω ☯

The Kailash Mountain is the abode of Shiva. His conjugal life is just taken off from there when the unwarranted and painful event of his beloved wife Sati's death occurs.

This place is full of different rare herbs, vegetables and is sanctified by Vedic hymns and mystic yoga practice.

The peace, tranquility and serenity of Kailash Hill are enchanting. One's mind smoothens by the rhythmical sound of the peacocks' sweet vibrations.

Bees' humming and cuckoo's singing make one seat in natures lap for eternal time.

There are trees which produce flowers with fragrant aromas. There are lakes with golden lotus flower.

Forests and bushes have cinnamon tree, malati, kubja, mallika, and Madhavi shrubs.

Mountains of Kailash have storage of jewels and minerals. Beautiful and varieties of deer, many waterfalls and caves are attractive features of these mountains.

The residents of the place are demigods by birth and have all mystic powers.

Besides them there are other human beings like the Kinnaras, Gandharvas and their beautiful wives, who are known as Apsaras or Angels.

There is a small lake named Alaknanda in which Sati used to take her bath. That lake is especially auspicious.

Every living beings of the Kailash stand lifeless in absence of Sati. Each and every corners of the Kailash are touched and irrigated by Devi Sati with her own hands. Much of those gardens, forests and bushes with flowers and fruits are appeared fainted in her absence.

There stands a very old great banyan tree casting a wide spread shade, cooling the ambient. Physically tired and mentally drained with pain and remembrance of Sati, grief-stricken Shiva prefers to sit under it alone.

He is sitting on straw mattress on a deerskin and is practicing all forms of austerity. Smeared with ashes his body looked like an evening cloud. On his matted hair is the sign of a half-moon, a symbolic representation.

Gradually saintly persons like Kuber, the master of the Guhyakas and the four Kumara, who were already liberated souls and great sage Narada, come to see Shiva.

They find bereaved Shiva seating with left leg placed on his right thigh and his left hand placed on his left thigh. This sitting posture is called virasana. In his right hand he is holding rudraksa beads and his finger is in the mode of argument.

Shiva once again goes back to ascetic form of life and detaches himself from the materialistic world.

ЖΨΦΩ ↂ

Chapter 14

Justice Served

Prajapati Daksha, the despot by his evil design had almost brought in catastrophic end to this world.

By his evil act he has precipitated in great mental and physical damages to all his well wishers who attended the Yajna.

After the destruction of the Yajna fear-driven priests, demigods and other traumatized members go to Brahmadev for help.

Brahmadev tells all the visitors, "By keeping Shiva excluded from the sacrifice you all are offender of blasphemes."

"With open heart and mind you all go to Shiva and surrender by falling down on his lotus feet" says Brahmadev.

Brahmadev accepts the fact that no one, not even himself, Indra and others present there has much idea about Shiva's power.

After advising the demigods he himself takes all of them with him and start for Shiva's abode Kailash.

ЖΨΦΩ☮

Sky of Kailash appears no bluer.

Mountain Kailash has lost its glory in absence of beloved Sati. It appears as if someone has snatched away all the happiness of the Shiva's abode, the beautiful Kailash.

Reaching Kailash all demi gods and others become amazed with the beauty peace and tranquility of the place particularly to those who are encountering it for the first time.

They are also struck with wonder at the great opulence to be found here.

Death of beloved Sati has torn off Shiva like a knife-ridden.

He becomes a madman, choosing annihilation.

But how does one annihilate something that has never born?

So, the universe has bore the brunt of Shiva's grief, in the form of destruction.

Even that couldn't liberate him from his grief. So Shiva embraces silence and turns within.

It leads to an unforeseen and miraculous expansion in Shiva from which Yoga is born.

Gods find Shiva sitting under a great old banyan tree, which is competent to give perfection to mystic yogis.

As grave as time eternal he appears to have given up all anger. He is seen surrounded by great saints and sages.

All the sages and demigods headed by Indra come forward and offer their respectful obeisances unto Shiva with folded hands.

As soon as Shiva notices Brahmadev among the demigods he immediately stands up and offers him respect by bowing down and touching his lotus feet.

Brahmadev has an inner satisfaction seeing Shiva in such a devastated mental and physical state after losing Sati.

Shiva's personal ascetic and spiritual life gets a big jolt with the loss of Goddess Sati's satvik power.

But Brahmadev hides that feeling of happiness and does not allow it to surface on his face.

He presents a usual smiling face and begins to speak, – "My dear Shiva, you are the controller of the entire material manifestation, the combined father and mother of the cosmic manifestation and the Supreme Brahman beyond the cosmic manifestation as well. You create this cosmic manifestation, maintain it, and annihilate it."

Brahmadev continues, "My dear for miscreants you have destined different kinds of hells which are horrible and ghastly. At the same time some devotees have fully dedicated their lives unto your lotus feet as Paramatma. Such persons treat all living entities equally. They never become overwhelmed by anger like animals."

"There are persons who observe everything with differentiation and criticising attitude. They are simply attached to fruitive activities and are mean-minded. They envy seeing the flourishing condition of others. Thus they give distress to them by uttering harsh and piercing words. Such persons have already been killed by providence. There is no need for them to be killed again by an exalted personality like you, my dear" says Brahmadev.

Brahmadev continues speaking to Shiva "My dear, if some materialists, bewildered by the insurmountable illusory energy of the Supreme Godhead commit offenses, a saintly person with compassion does not take this seriously. Knowing that they commit offences because they are overpowered by the illusory energy, saintly person does not show his prowess to counteract them.

My dear, you are never bewildered by the formidable influence of the illusory energy of the Supreme Personality of Godhead. Therefore you are omniscient and should be merciful and compassionate towards them".

Brahmadev continues "My dear Shiva, you are a shareholder of a portion of the sacrifice and you are the giver of the result. The bad priests have not delivered your share and therefore you have destroyed everything and the sacrifice has remained unfinished. Now you can do the needful and take your rightful share".

Further he prays with folding hands "My dear, by your mercy the performer of the sacrifice, King Daksha may get back his life, Bhaga may get back his eyes, Bhrigu his mustache, and Pusa his teeth. O Shiva may the demigods and the priests whose limbs have been broken by your soldiers recover from the injuries by your grace. O destroyer of the sacrifice, please take your portion of the sacrifice and let the sacrifice be completed by your grace".

Shiva hears long prayer of Brahmadev patiently and carefully.

He looks apparently calmed and pacified.

Shiva decides to lend justice in place.

He replies saying "My dear father Brahmadev I do not mind the offenses created by the demigods as they are childish and less intelligent. I do not take a serious view of their offenses. I have punished them only in order to right them."

He then pronounces "Since the head of Daksha has already been burnt to ashes, he will have the head of a goat."

He continues with his giveaways, "Demigod named Bhaga will be able to see his share of sacrifice through the eyes of Mitra.

Demigod Pusa will be able to chew only through the teeth of his disciples and if alone he will have to satisfy himself by eating dough made from chickpea flour.

Demigods who have agreed to give me my share of the sacrifice will recover from all their injuries.

Those who have had their arms cut off will have to work with the arms of Ashwini Kumara.

Those whose hands are cut off will have to do their work with the hands of Pusa. The priests will also have to act in that manner.

As for Bhrigu he will have the beard from the goat's head."

Benevolent Shiva resolves the issues rose in the aftermath of Devi Sati's death.

All the personalities present are seemed very much satisfied in heart and soul upon hearing the words of Shiva, the best among the benedictors.

ЖΨΦΩↀ

Thereafter on the invitation of Sage Bhrigu, Shiva and Brahmadev accompanied with all demigods return to the place where the great sacrifice is being performed.

After everything gets executed exactly as directed by Shiva, Daksha's body is joined to the head of the Goat, an animal meant to be killed in the sacrifice.

King Daksha with the head of a goat is then brought to consciousness.

As he wakes up from sleep, the King sees Shiva standing before him.

He wants to offer prayers to Shiva. But as he remembers the ill-fated death of his daughter Sati his eyes fills with tears.

In bereavement his voice gets choked up. He is not able to say anything. With great endeavor he reconciles himself and with pure consciousness begins to offer prayers to Shiva.

Goat-face King Daksha says "My dear Shiva, I have committed a great offense against you. But you are so kind that instead of withdrawing your mercy, you have done me a great favor by punishing me. You and Vishnu never neglect even useless unqualified Brahmanas. Why should you neglect me, who am engaged in performing sacrifices?"

Daksha continues "My dear great and powerful Shiva you are created to protect the Brahmanas in pursuing education, austerities, vows and self-realization. As protector of the Brahmanas, you always protect the regulative principles they follow, just as a cowherd boy keeps a stick in his hand to give protection to the cows.

I did not know your full glories. For this reason, I threw arrows of sharp words at you in the open assembly, although you did not take them into account. I was going down to hell because of my disobedience to you. You are the most respectable personality and took compassion upon me and saved me by awarding punishment. I request that you be pleased by your own mercy since I cannot satisfy you by my words."

Shiva pardons Daksha and the Yajna restarts.

Soon Vishnu appears there in His original form as Narayana.

Following the due spiritual ritualistic offerings and the procedure, the infamous Yajna is finally completed.

Ж Ψ Φ Ω ↀ

Chapter 15

The Mystery of Divine Connection

Uninvited Sati's presence in Yajna arena at Kanakhala has irritated the host Prajapati Daksha.

Instead of welcoming her daughter Daksha yells at her. He snubs her with volley of insults targeting her and Shiva.

Insults becoming unbearable, angry Sati transform her to the form of Goddess Ad Parashakti. Her appearance with three eyes, eight hands carrying Trishul, shield, mace, bow, arrow, chakra, long sword and one hand as Abhaya mudra make Her look ferocious. Entire population present get struck with her effulgence and become spell-bound.

After introducing herself as Eternal Power She curses Daksha and all gods and goddesses who have provoked him in this secret game, to be killed. She curses the Yajna ritual to remain incomplete and that Tamas would subdue its Sattvik nature.

She declared before immolating herself in the Yajna fire that she renounced all the mortal relationships, nothing bound her. She gave her final salutations to her husband Shiva and to her mother. Then she prayed that she be reborn to a father, whom she could respect.

So saying, Devi Sati immolated her mortal body through the invocation of her yogic powers. As the Tatva of Shakti left the mortal shell, the mortal body of Devi Sati collapsed to the floor in scorching flames.

Upon learning about Sati's terrible death Shiva was sorrow but furious on Daksha Prajapati. In his wrath he invoked his power to ensure killing of Daksha and his associates with complete destruction of the Yajna.

Shiva went into inconsolable grief when he saw the half burnt corpse of his beloved wife. Out of grief and sorrow, Shiva carried Sati's body on his shoulder, reminiscing about their moments of love and happiness as a couple.

Angry Shiva roamed around the universe, performing the fearsome and awe-inspiring Rudra Tandava dance. Shiva unable to part with Sati took her corpse and continued wandering.

Brahmadev, the producer and director of the Divine Event was smiling inside his mind as his plan had succeeded. Shiva was hurt at his weakest point and he could take his revenge.

But he was unmindful of what was happening to the world. The Universe was on the brink of destruction by Shiva's Tandav Nritya.

ЖΨΦΩↀ

Unable to bear the fury of the Shiva's dance, all demigods afraid of the ensuing danger, approached Vishnu to intervene.

In order to calm Shiva he activated his divine disc "Sudarshan Chakra" and severed Sati's body in to pieces.

The severed pieces of Sati's corpse are believed to have landed in the places wherever Shiva roamed carrying her corpse on his shoulder. The places where the body parts of Sati Devi's corpse fall become very sacred places to the Hindus.

The devotees and worshippers of Goddess Adi Parashakti or Adi Shakti or Mahadevi consider this Divine incidence as Goddess's willingness to make her abode on the earth.

Falling of severed body parts are the means by which her divine connection with this world of mankind is established. These places remain eternally as the source of Divine Energy. Shaivites in general and the Shaktas in particular promptly recognise this Divine incidence. Their sacred belief in the power of Adi Shakti allow them to realise Goddess Adi Shakti has wanted this way. They term these places as the abode of Goddess Adi Parashakti. They consider these places as the Centers of Divine Energy. Hindus built temple for worshipping her in these sacred places. These sacred places of worship come to be popularly known as Shakti Peeths. Each of the Shaktipeeth has also got Shiva as her saviour or protector. These Divine destinations, the Shaktipeeths had come into being in the Hindu religion since the time of Satya Yuga.

Kanakhala, a place on the earth thus become the epicenter of the mystery which constitutes this creation of the Shaktipeeths i.e. the Abode of Adi Shakti on the earth through the above Divine incidence. It is these Centres of Divine Energy through which Goddess Adi Parashakti or Adi Shakti or Mahadevi connects herself with her devotees on the earth. This significant divine event has happened at Kanakhala and hence it draws its name as Kanakhala mystery. The Divine event of Kanakhala thus remains as the mysterious reason for the creation of Shaktipeeth.

Ж Ψ Φ Ω ↂ

In unraveling the mystery in a more simplified manner we would rather assume that the Human world is the play ground of the Gods and Goddesses. Trimurti is considered as most worshipped Gods among the Hindus. These three Gods more often indulge in run up play for increasing the number of their worshippers in the human world. The event containing the sequence Brahmadev – Daksha – Sati – Vishnu – Shiva as major actors is considered to have been one such Hindu mythological saga. Here the hidden role of the Trimurti is clearly visible. One of the Trimurtis wanted to hurt another. For doing so he utilised the services of a dedicated worshipper of the third of the Trimurti. Foundation of the Divine destination, the Center of Divine Energy is the ultimate outcome of such a great mythological misadventure drama that was played amongst the Trimurtis themselves.

Mysterious event was conceptualised by Brahmadev at his abode Satyaloka. Brahmadev felt that Shiva had been the reason for many of his embarrassments faced in his first Kalpa (Pitri Kalpa) when the universe was formed. So he waited for the suitable occasion to embarrass Shiva.

The dreamer Brahmadev, the Operator dreamt of a plan to cause immense loss to Shiva. The entire plan drawn in the Satyaloka is given the final shape at the Kanakhala Sacrifice arranged by Daksha Prajapati.

Brahmadev used Prajapati Daksha, one of his mind-sons for the job. Daksha was the dedicated devotee of Vishnu and was not acquainted much with Shiva's power. In fact Daksha possessed deep hatred for Shiva. This factor worked in Brahmadev's favour to choose Daksha as the central character.

Brahmadev himself got Goddess Adi Shakti incarnated as daughter Sati to Daksha and got her married to Shiva.

Then he made Daksha as the Head of the Prajapatis. To celebrate this auspicious occasion Daksha organised a huge Yajna under the supervision of Brahmadev.

In this yajna Daksha invited all Kings or Prajapatis, Demigods, Rishis, Sages together with their families. But he did not invite his own daughter Sati and son-in-law Shiva possibly out of his extreme hatred for him.

Brahmadev knew that this would not bear well for the Yajna but preferred to maintain silence. Brahmadev was engaged in his own world of arrogance and jealousy. He perhaps did not visualise what His son's mischievous action (which had his placid support) was about to accomplish.

We have known what happened subsequently in the Yajna arena.

ЖΨΦΩↂ

Hindu Puranas accepted that Sati's body was dismembered by the Vishnu's Sudarshan Chakra into 51 pieces which fell on earth at various places.

Hindu Scholars identified these 51 holy Centers of Divine Energy as the abode of Goddess Adi Parashakti created on Earth. These Divine Energy centres are destinations where all powerful Divine Mother Goddess Adi Shakti is worshipped.

These Divine destinations are revered and maintained by the Goddess Adi Parashakti worshippers of Shakta sect. Through Divine Mother Goddess Adi Shakti they worship Shakti or Power. This is the reason why these Centers of Divine Energy are also named as the Shaktipeeths.

Entirely all of her body parts were the symbolism of each manifestation of Goddess Adi-Parashakti. Bhairav has incarnated himself to protect her Shaktipeeths in different forms for the fortification from the evil forces. So we find every Shaktipeeth having temple of her consort Shiva in his various form. Some of these Shaktipeeths are also having Jyotirling Shrines of Shiva attached to them.

Incidence of Daksha Yajna, the death of Goddess Adi Parashakti in her incarnation as Sati and creation of Shaktipeeths are all the episodes happened in Brahmadev's first Kalpa when the universe was first evolved. Since then the mystery of the Shaktipeeths continued to enchant Hindu minds.

The Divine disc of Vishnu detached Sati's corpse from Shiva and controlled his destructive impulses. But the dismembered body parts of Devi Sati fell on the Earth which led to the development of the concept of Shaktipeeths and thereby strengthened Shaktism. Most significantly this aspect was not foreseen by Vishnu. Vishnu perhaps did not visualise that his action would give birth to the Abodes of Goddess Adi Parashakti on the Earth. His action was solely aimed to save the Universe. But it turned out to become the reason for propagation of the Shaktism. This underlying truth hidden in the Kanakhala mystery stands unraveled as well.

Daksha's Yajna and Devi Sati's death became an important event in Shaivism. It is the story behind the 'Stala Purana' (Origin story of Temples) of the mystery of the Shakti Peethas. Vishnu's humanitarian action forms the basis of the establishment of the Shakti Peethas, the Centers of Divine Energy or the temples of the Hindu Divine Mother. Kanakhala stood as the witness of the Divine mystery which constitutes the creation of the Abodes of Goddess Adi Shakti on the earth through the series of complex divine events. Secrecy associated with the commonly known Shaktipeeths thus opened up to us.

The mythological event is mainly told in the Vayu Purana. It is also mentioned in the Kasi Kanda of the Skanda Purana, the Kurma Purana, Harivamsa Purana and Padma Purana. In addition Linga Purana, Shiva Purana, and Matsya Purana also detail the incident.

ЖΨΦΩↀ

Chapter 16

Significance of Shaktipeeth

Hindu beliefs revere the feminine form of Divinity as the manifestation of energy – Shakti.

Adi Parashakti or the Adi Shakti or the Mahadevi, the Mother Goddess, is considered to be the personification of Cosmic Energy in its dynamic form.

It is believed that Adi Shakti is the power and energy with which the Universe is created, preserved, destroyed and recreated (through her command by the trinity of Hinduism – Brahmadev, Vishnu and Shiva).

Parvati, who became the consort of Shiva after 21 Manvantara since Goddess Sati's death, or Lakshmi the consort of Vishnu are enshrined in temples all over India. Some of these shrines are also considered as Shakti Peeths in the same degree of faith as associated with the abode of Goddess Adi Shakti.

Many other ancient shrines closely tied to local legends and beliefs. Such temples have become an integral part of Indian tantric tradition. Some of these shrines are also considered as Shakti Peeths, where Hindu Tantrics worship the primeval source of energy – Shakti in the form of Mother Goddess Adi Parashakti or Mahadevi.

Shakti is worshipped in several forms. As Rajarajeshwara or Kamakshi, she is the Universal mother. As Uma or Parvati, she is the gentle consort of Shiva. As Meenakshi – she is the queen of Shiva. As Durga she rides the tiger and bears weaponry. In the angry and terrifying form of Kali, she destroys and devours all forms of evil.

Belief in Shakti or the feminine aspect of Divinity is an integral and popular element of the religious fabric of the entire subcontinent. Female guardian deities are revered in all parts of India.

ЖΨΦΩↂ

The Shakta Agama deals with the worship protocol adhered to in Devi temples. There is a shrine to Shakti in virtually all Saivites temples throughout the Indian Sub-continent. Tantric practices involving chants, gestures and tantras (geometric shapes) also govern the worship of Shakti.

Centers of Divine Energy or the Shakti Peethas are sacred abodes of Goddess Adi Parashakti in both her incarnation as Sati and as Parvati. Like Devi Sati, Parvati too is aspect of the Goddess Adi Parashakti, who helped Shiva, come away from his ascetic isolation and involve himself in Samsara (the material world). She is equally fiery with a frightening temper but also loving and extremely benevolent by nature.

Goddess Adi Shakti took her incarnation as Sati in the first Manvantara. After Sati's death Shiva lived without the Shakti aspect of Adi Shakti for a period of 21 Manvantara (14 in Pitri Kalpa and 7 in Varaha Kalpa).

After this long interval, Adi Shakti was reborn as Parvati, a daughter to Himavan, king of mountains and his wife Menavati. She is also known as Uma or Hemavati. This time Adi Shakti was born as the daughter of a father whom she could respect, a father who was an ardent follower of Shiva. In her incarnation as Devi Parvati Goddess Adi Shakti once again accepted Shiva as her husband.

Followers of Shaktism the Shaktas worship Goddess Adi Shakti in both the form of 'Sati' and or 'Parvati' at the Shaktipeeths. Shakta worshippers pursued their objectives through Tantric practices through the ages, centuries and Yugas.

Many regional rulers and kings have followed Goddess Adi Shakti as source of power. They have built temples in those sacred places. They helped these sacred places in becoming famous through their patronage. These shrines are symbol of mother strength derived from Goddess Adi-Parashakti.

These shrines are scattered all over Indian sub-continent. Out of 51 Shaktipeeths 10 Shaktipeeths are situated outside India. Those countries are Sri Lanka (1), Bangladesh (4), Nepal (3), Tibet (1) and Pakistan (1). Of the 41 Shaktipeeths 16 are located in the Eastern region, 8 in the northern, 5 in the western, 7 in the southern and 5 in the central India.

Out of 51 Shaktipeeths, 18 are said to be Maha Shakti Peeths (Annexure I). At all the Shakti Peeths, the Goddess Shakti is accompanied by her consort, Bhairava (a manifestation of Shiva).

Great religious texts viz., the Shiva Purana, the Devi Bhagavata, the Kalika Purana and the AstaShakti recognize four Shakti Peeths as Adi Shakti Peeths. They are: (1) Bimala (Pada Khanda) located in the complex of Jagannath temple of Puri, Odisha, (2) Tara Tarini (Sthana Khanda, Purnagiri, Breasts) located near Berhampur, Ganjam in Odisha, (3) Kamakhya Temple (Yoni Khanda) located near Guwahati, Assam and (4) Dakshina Kalika (Mukha Khanda) located at Kolkata, West Bengal. These shrines are identified to be as ancient as the Satya Yuga. Indian Mythology completes a full circle and brings in the Shaktipeeths, the Centers of Divine Energy.

ЖΨΦΩↀ

PART II

The Travelogue

Divine Abode of Adi Shakti or the Centers of Divine Energy, commonly known as the Shaktipeeths on the earth are in existence in reality since time immemorial. Started as the centers of worship of Goddess Adi Shakti by the 'Shakta' sect of the Shaivites these become sacred temples for Hindus in general through the Yuga and centuries. Regional rulers and kings worshipped the Goddess as the source of power. They built temples at her Abode on Earth and popularised these sacred Divine Energy centres amongst masses over a long period. Underlying spirituality of the Kanakhala connection have been motivating people to roam around these Divine destinations for a long time. Being a vivid traveller I took to roaming amidst the Shaktipeeths in search of divine connection. Some of these travel stories constitute the Travelogue. This contains 18 sub-sections comprising my travel that spread over far flung area of my country – from east/north-east to the far-west and from north to far-south. My overwhelming experience of touring in the Shaktipeeths has encountered face to face the depth of obedience, besieged faith and dependence of people on the Divine Mother. As observed my encounter is difficult to elaborate in words. That is more of a matter of one's feelings within. That is "Seeing believes". I believe in the truth behind each of this temple that goes in uplifting the moral power in oneself.

Devi Kamakhya

We are just shifted to Guwahati on transfer. It is absolutely a new place for my family. Local language is Assamese which apparently sounds in ear close to Bengali but there are a few marked deviations.

After we settled down in Guwahati, we planned on a Sunday to pay our reverence to Devi Kamakhya, at the famous Kamakhya temple. It is one of the 51 Shaktipeeths and is also one of the four Adi Shaktipeeths. The temple is situated on the edge of the Neelachal hills top at the height of approx. 800 ft and is about 12 kms from the Guwahati city centre.

We hired a local taxi for a whole day trip of the Guwahati city. First stoppage was at Kamakhya Temple. After driving towards the western part of the city for about half an hour on the Guwahati Airport road, our car took a left hand turn to enter into a hilly track. Soon the car reached height and the Guwahati city appeared in the form of birds eye view. The Neelachal hills itself was very picturesque and the surrounding sceneries equally fascinating. Soon we reached the top of the hills. Driver parked the car. We went up to the temple complex to notice a long queue of men and women waiting to pay their reverence to the Goddess.

Fortunately my friend at Guwahati got us a guiding priest with entry permission ready. With him we walked down the stairs to reach the temple complex which was at a lower plane.

Temple complex (**Fig 1**) is found to be huge. Beside the main 'Kamakhya' Temple there are ten more individual temples dedicated to the ten Mahavidyas viz. Kali, Tara, Tripurasundari or Shodashi, Bhuvaneshwari, Bhairavi, Chhinnamasta, Dhumavati, Bagalamukhi, Matangi and Kamala. We are given to understand that the temple structure undergone reconstruction and renovation many times during the period 8th to 17th century. The last renovation gave rise to this present hybrid indigenous style known as the Neelachal type.

Entire temple consists of four chambers – the Garbhagriha with a hemispherical dome on a cruciform base to which three Mandapas locally called Calanta, Pancharatna and Natamandira are aligned from east to west. Architecture of the Garbhagriha reflect combination of construction types – the base plinth similar to that of the Surya Temple at Tezpur, dados on the top of the plinth with sunken panels similar to that of central Indian style of the Khajuraho. The panels have delightful sculptured Ganesha and other Hindu gods and goddesses. The lower portion is made of stone while the Shikhara in the shape of a polygonal beehive-like dome is made of brick. The Shikhara is circled by a number of minaret inspired Angashikharas of Bengal type Charchala. The Shikhara, Angashikharas and other chambers were built in the 16th century and after.

The inner sanctum i.e., the Garbhagriha is below the ground level. We walked down a narrow steep cave like zone a few steps below to enter the Garbhagriha. The passage was very narrow and also a bit dark inside. Only 2-3 small lamps are seen there inside the cave, so it is very hard to see anything clearly. At this point all queues are joined giving rise to a milieu.

Prior to entering the temple my wife had bought puja offerings flowers and leaves, etc. Typical offerings included a coconut, a packet of lachidana, a chunri, a small box of sindoor and some incense sticks. We finally reached near the sanctum sanctorum. We found there was no image or idol. Inside the cave there was a flat mound of stone or rock fissure that sloped downwards from both sides meeting in a yoni-like depression some 10 inches deep. This hollow ridge below the ground level was constantly filled with water from an underground perennial spring. It is the vulva-shaped depression that is being worshiped as the goddess Kamakhya herself, the key Deity. It is considered as most important abode of the Devi Adi Shakti. The ridge usually remains covered with the flowers and other offerings. Generally, it's very difficult to see that rock fissure because of the darkness. The Priest was helpful and enabled us to touch Holi depression. It was a moment as if a divine wisdom engulfed us. Our eyes got closed with reverence to Devi Adi Shakti Mata 'Kamakhya'. We then spent few minutes more inside there.

For a while we were out of the worries amidst the peace and serenity of the sanctum sanctorum. We then came out of the temple as persons with totally different feeling.

'Kamakhya' Devi Temple is believed to be 2000 years old. In such a long existence, it was destroyed and rebuilt several times. The current structure is about 500 years old. The Adhistana of the temple indicates that the original temple was of Nagara style. Old stone Shikhara was renovated and replaced by the present brick structure in the 16th century. Part of the Antarala is of Aathchala type. Amongst the three additional chambers the first situated towards the west was the Calanta, a square chamber of type Aathchala (very similar to the 1659 AD built Radha-Vinod Temple of Bishnupur). The entrance to the temple through its northern door is of Ahom type dochala. The walls of this chamber contain sculpted images of Naranarayana, related inscriptions and other gods. It leads into the Garbhagriha via descending steps. To the west of Calanta were large and rectangular Pancharatna with a flat roof and five smaller Shikhara of the same style as the main Shikara. The middle Shikhara is slightly bigger than the other four. The last chamber i.e. the natamandira extends to the west of the Pancharatna with an apsidal end and ridged roof of the Ranghar type Ahom style. Inscriptions on the inner wall indicated that this structure was built between 1759 and 1782 AD.

Mata 'Kamakhya' Devi Temple is a major center for Tantric Worshippers. It is the place where the yoni (vagina) of Goddess Sati fell from her burnt corpse severed by the Sudarshan Chakra during the Tandav Nritya (dance) of Lord Shiva. This place is one of the four principle abodes of Goddess Adi Shakti, known as Adi Shaktipeeth.

Kamakhya Temple was established by King Bhagadatta Shashanka in the 7th century AD. This place has been mentioned in Kalika Purana and Rudrayamala Tantra as a famous pilgrimage site dedicated to Shakti worship. The Mlechchha dynasty (650–900 AD) ruled Kamrupa from their capital at Harruppesvar in present-day Tezpur, Assam, after the fall of the Varman dynasty. History of Kamrup Kamakhya goes as old as 9th century as per the epigraphic notice found in the 9th-century Tezpur plates of Vanamalavarmadeva of the Mlechchha dynasty. From Indra Pala to Dharma Pala the last of the Pala dynasty were followers of the Tantrik tenet. During their time Kamakhya became an important seat of Tantrikism. As stated in the Kalika Purana composed in the 10th century AD, Kamakhya became a renowned centre of Tantrik sacrifices, mysticism and sorcery.

Kamakhya temple was destroyed during Hussein Shah's invasion of the Kamata kingdom in the medieval India in 1498 AD. The ruins of the temple were then discovered by Vishwasingha

(1515–1540 AD), the founder of the Koch dynasty. He revived worshipping at the site. The temple was reconstructed in 1565 AD by his son Nara Narayan (1540–1587 AD). Later rulers of Ahom kingdom further renovated the temple. The current final structure was rebuilt during the Ahom times, with remnants of the earlier Koch temple carefully preserved.

As per an interesting legend still valid, there caused some disruption in the maintenance of the temple later days. Koch Bihar royal family was cursed by Devi herself restraining them from offering puja at the temple. In fear of this curse even to this day no descendants of that family dare to look upward towards the Kamakhya hill while passing by. In the absence of the Koch royal family support the temple faced lot of hardship. When King Jayadhvaj Singha conquered Kamrup in 1658 AD his interests in the temple grew. The decades that followed the Ahom kings, all who were either devout Shaivite or Shakta continued to support the temple by rebuilding and renovating it.

Rudra Singha (reign 1696 to 1714 AD) at his old age decided to become an orthodox Hindu. Under the care of Krishnaram Bhattacharyya, a famous Mahant of Shakta sect from Nadia district of Bengal, he became an orthodox Hindu. King made his spiritual Guru the independent caretaker of the temple. After the death of Rudra Singha, his eldest son Shiba Singha (reign 1714 to 1744 AD) handed over the management of the Kamakhya temple along with the large areas of land (Debottar land) to Mahant Krishnaram Bhattacharyya. The Mahant and his successors resided on top of the Neelachal hill. Current day priests are either disciples or descendants of the Parbatiya Gosains.

The Kalika Purana describes Devi Kamakhya as who fulfils all desire and gives salvation. Symbolic to this the temple has a special form of Sindoor made from the Neelachal rock. Local people believe it to be a blessing bestowed by Kamakhya Devi herself to the wearer of this sindoor. Tantra remained basic to worship, in the precincts of this ancient temple of mother goddess Kamakhya. Another interesting legend as per the Kalika Purana still prevail that Kamakhya Temple denotes the spot where Dakshanayani Sati used to retire in secret to satisfy her amour with Shiva.

Kamakhya temple was the very first Shaktipeeth that we visited. We were in the lap of Devi 'Kamakhya' which left indelible and everlasting imprint in our mind and soul.

Dakshina Kali

That was the time we had completed one year of stay in Kolkata post my retirement.

One day we decided to visit Goddess Dakshina Kali at Kalighat temple to pay our reverence. This is a Hindu temple dedicated to the Goddess Kali, an incarnation of Goddess Adi Parashakti. It is one of the four Adi Shaktipeeths.

Kalighat is one of the oldest neighbourhoods in South Kolkata, densely populated. It has the history of cultural intermingling with the various foreign incursions into the area over time.

Long ago Kalighat was a Ghat (landing stage) on the main course of the Hooghly River (local name of the River Bhagirathi) in the city of Calcutta. The main river over a period of time moved away leaving the present form of a narrow canal behind. The Holi temple is now on the bank of this canal, which connects to the Hooghly. The Canal was the original course of the river Hoogly and hence it was once named as the local Adi Ganga.

Mention of Kalighat temple is available in the 15th century texts viz. Manasar Bhasan and the 17th century texts of Kavi Mukundadas's Chandi Mangal. Mention of the Kali temple is also found in Lalmohon Bidyanidhis's "Sambanda Nirnoy".
The original temple was a small hut. The Medieval Bhuiyan, Raja Basanta Ray, uncle of Pratapaditya and the King of Jessore, (now in

Bangladesh) probably built the first Temple here. This temple was situated on the bank of river Adi Ganga.

The present temple was built by the Sabarna Roy Choudhury family of Barisha in 1809. They offered 595 bighas of land to the Temple deity so that worship and service could be continued smoothly. Historically, traders bating on the river Hooghly halted at Kalighat to pay patronage to the goddess.

The present day Dakshina Kali idol is made of touchstone. This was created in 1570 CE by two saints – Brahmananda Giri and Atmaram Giri based on the idol of Mata Bhuvaneshwari, the Kuladevi of Sabarna Roy Choudhury family. It was Padmabati Devi, the mother of Laksmikanta Roy Choudhury who discovered the fossils of Sati's finger in a lake called Kalikunda. This discovery made Kalighat as one of the 51 Shakti Pithas.

The layout of the temple Complex is interesting one. The natmandir, a hall attached to the Garbhagriha sanctum sanctorum is in the southern wing while Shiva's temple is situated in the north-eastern wing. There is a temple dedicated to Radha Krishna built in 1843 AD by a Zamindar of Bhaowali. The Kalighat temple in its present form is only about 200 years old.

On the desired day we arrived at the temple. There are four entries to the temple complex. We preferred to enter through the main gate on the southern side. First my wife bought the Puja offering items from the nearest stall. Through the same stall we got in touch with a Priest guide who agreed to take us to the temple for Darshan and Puja.

He took us through a separate short-cut passage. Soon we were standing before the Goddess. We found that the image of Goddess Kali in this temple was unique (**Fig 2**). It did not follow the pattern of other Kali images in Bengal.

The Idol was of touchstone and was told to be created by two saints viz. Atmaram Brahmachari and Brahmananda Giri. We saw that the idol's three huge eyes, a long protruding tongue and four hands were all made of gold. Out of the four hands, the top left hand holds a Kharga or a Scimitar, the bottom left holds a severed head of the Asura King *Shumbha*, while the top right hand she shows the Abhay Mudra, and the bottom right hands she shows the Varada Mudra.

Whilst the Scimitar signifies Divine Knowledge, the severed head of the Asura signifies the human Ego which has to be slain by the Divine Knowledge to attain Moksha or one's goal in life. The Abhay Mudra signifies that the Goddess is always there with her devotees, protecting them from harm. The Varada Mudra represents the benevolence and the soft-heartedness of the Devi. This showers her devotees with divine and material blessings, which means any devotee worshiping her with a true heart will be saved as she will guide them here and hereafter.

Our priest helped us in offering our Puja prayers through necessary formalities. We handed over our flowers and others to the head priest who was standing inside. The Priest made us utter a few Sanskrit slokas for Devi along with him and offered our reverence with folded hands. Then he returned Prasad to us. We stood before the Goddess for some more time in silence and with complete reverence. We felt an all conquering feeling within us. We moved out of the main temple precinct and walked down in the complex courtyard. We came across a few important places viz., Soshtitala, Natmandir, Jor-Bangla, Hari-Kath Tala, Radha Krishna temple and Kundupukur. Kundupukur is the sacred tank situated in the south-east of the temple outside the boundary walls. The 'Sati-Ango' (the right toe of Sati) was discovered from this tank. The tank could not be emptied signifying the possibility of a subterranean link with the Adi Ganga. The Temple at Kalighat is revered as an important Shakti Peetha, by the Shakta sect of Hinduism. The Shakti here is the Dakshina Kali, while the Bhairav being Nakuleshwar. Some Puranas also mention that the Mukha Khanda or the face of the Goddess fell here, got fossilized, and is stored and worshipped here. It is given to believe that the 51 Shakti Peethas are linked to the 51 alphabets in Sanskrit, each carrying the power to invoke one of the goddesses associated with them. These Alphabets are called Veej Mantras or the seeds of the primordial sounds of creation. The Veej Mantra for Dakshina Kali is Kring. We bowed our heads on the feet of Devi Dakshina Kali and received her blessings.

Vimala

We were posted in Kolkata then.

Our son has become five year old. We decided to visit Puri to spend our holidays there.

Puri in the eastern India is one of the four Dhams associated with Vishnu, others three being Dwarka in the west, Badrinath in the north and Rameswaram in the south.

We did not know about the presence of one of the Adi Shakti Peeths there when we planned our visit. It was only after completing our offerings to Lord Jagannath that we came to know that Puri is also considered as a Shaktipeeth. It was the abode of Goddess Adi-Parashakti too. This temple of Devi Sati is locally known as the Vimala (or Bimala) Temple. It is located in the same complex.

After paying our reverence to Jagannath we walked down towards the south-west corner of the inner enclosure of the temple complex. Then we crossed the sacred Kund known as Rohini Kund on the western corner of the tower of Jagannath, and reached the Vimala Temple.

The Vimala temple is important to the Goddess-oriented Shakti and Tantra worshippers. Goddess Vimala is said to be considered as the Tantric consort of Jagannath and a guardian of the temple complex. Devotees pay respect to Vimala before worshipping Jagannath in the main temple. Food offered to Jagannath does not get sanctified as Mahaprasad until it is also offered to Goddess Vimala.

While walking in complex we found that the temple face was to the east. Construction appears to be of sandstone and laterite. The architecture is said to be of Deula style. There were four compartments – Vimana or the Garbhagriha (the sanctum sanctorum), jagamohana (the assembly hall), nata-mandapa (the festival hall) and bhoga-mandapa (hall of offerings). Overall size of the shrine appeared to relatively smaller in the entire complex.

We reached the entrance of the Shrine outside the Bhoga Mandapa. There is a 4 feet Gaja-Simha, the lion riding over an elephant, symbolizing the victory of good over evil. It is covered by a flat roof. We entered the Bhoga Mandapa. It is a square shape hall on a high platform with a high roof. On the inner wall we noticed an eight-armed dancing Ganesha and a 12-armed, six-headed standing Kartikeya. The bhoga mandapa has four doorways guarded by two female gatekeepers. Through the flight of steps at the eastern doorway we reached the main entrance of the temple. We then passed through the Nata mandapa which is a large rectangular room. It housed the vimana and jagamohana. The room stands on a platform and the top is having a small pyramidal pinnacle. Inner walls are adorned with traditional paintings, depicting sixteen forms of the Hindu Goddess, including the Mahavidyas. Through one of the four doors we reached the Jagamohana or Mukhasala.

Mukhasala is a square building with a pyramid-shaped roof and a square base. The building stands on a high platform and outer wall is decorated with floral designs and scrollwork. The top has a pyramidal Shikhara but the inner walls have no ornamentation. The jagamohana had two doorways. Through one door we came out and then climbed up a few stairs to step into the sanctum sanctorum or Vimana. The lintel has the Gaja Lakshmi figurine in the centre surrounded with Apsaras (celestial maidens). The Navagraha (deities of the classical planets) are carved above the lintel. The doorjambs are decorated scrollwork, creepers, flowers and boys playing. Two gate-keeper sculptors surround the door. The Vimana is built in a Rekha deula style (a tall building with a shape of sugarloaf) and is said to be 60 feet in height with a 15 feet square base. It has a 2 feet platform decorated with lotus and other floral designs and scrollwork.

Within the Vimana is situated the Garbhagriha (sanctum), which was topped with a *pancharatha* – style, curvilinear temple pinnacle. Goddess Vimala is deified within the sanctum. The sanctum was the sixth century inner chamber and was devoid of wall decorations. The central icon of Goddess Vimala is installed on a simhasana (lion-throne), adorned with the figures of the goddess' female attendants Chhaya and Maya on the sides. The image is said to be made of *lakha* (a type of wax) and slightly taller than 4 feet.

We reached and stood before the image of the goddess (**Fig 3**). The icon is seen holding a rosary in the upper right hand. Her lower right hand is in a boon-giving gesture, lower left holds a pitcher considered to be filled with Amrita (celestial elixir of life) and the upper left hand is seen holding a naga-pasha (serpent-noose) in the hand. We stood silently for a while before the Goddess and offered our reverence to the Supreme Being. Then we came out through the other door of the sanctum.

The Devi Purana mentions this Abode of Goddess Adi Shakti as the Pada Khanda Shaktipeeth. It is believed as the place where feet of Sati fell. We understood that generally no separate food offerings are cooked for the goddess Vimala. The vegetarian food offerings to Jagannath are first offered to Vimala, after which they are sanctified as Mahaprasad. The Mahaprasad consists of dried rice mixed with grated coconut, cheese, curd and butter. The Shankaracharya, head of the Govardhana matha, receives a pot of the Mahaprasad and a plate of Khichdi that is offered to the presiding goddess (Adi-Shakti) of the matha as well as of the temple.

We generally have Bhairava as the guardian of the presiding goddess of the Shaktipeeth. In this case Jagannath (Krishna an avatar of Vishnu) is fulfilling that duty. Thus Goddess Vimala is also considered as Lakshmi, the consort of Vishnu. Conversely, Tantrics consider Jagannath as Shiva-Bhairava, rather than a form of Vishnu. So, in this temple complex, Vishnu is equated with Shiva which signifies the oneness of God. Vimala is identified with the goddesses Katyayini, Durga, Bhairavi, Bhuvaneshvari and Ekanamsha. She is considered the Shakti of Vishnu as well as Shiva. Puranas and various Tantra mentions this Shaktipeeth as the most sacred Adi Shaktipeeth. The people of Orissa take pride in the Vimala temple. It is prescribed that devotees pay their respects to the goddess Vimala before worshipping Jagannath in the main temple.

Historically saying the central icon of Goddess Vimala is of the sixth century AD. But the outside architecture resembled to the shrine of Narasimha near the *Mukti-mandapa* (a temple hall) in the Jagannath temple complex which was dated to the ninth century. The Madala Panji (sacred time table) stated that the temple was constructed by Yayati Keshari (c 922 – 1040), ruler of Somavashi Dynasty of South Kosala. The sculptures of the Vimala temple reflected the Somavashi style and might have been the part of the original temple, on whose ruins the new temple was constructed. Thus Vimala temple is believed to have preceded even the central Jagannath shrine. Our being at the feet of Mata 'Vimala' filled our mind and soul with unforgettable and everlasting joy and happiness which often rekindle our memory.

Tara Tarini

After retirement we have now permanently settled down at our home in Kolkata.

In the month of September relatively recent one, we planned to spend our holidays at Gopalpur on Sea. In one of the sight-seeing trip in that tour we visited Lake Chilika and the Tara Tarini Temple.

Hindus regard Temple Tara Tarini as one of the four Adi Shaktipeeths, Holi Abodes of the Adi-Parashakti Mother Goddess.

It is one of the oldest pilgrimage centers and is situated on the Kumari Hills at the bank of the River Rushikulya. When Vishnu's Sudarshan Chakra severed half burnt corpse of Sati from the shoulder of Shiva during his Tandava Nritya, Devi's breasts are believed to have fallen here. The Shakti of the shrine is addressed as Maa Tara Devi. The location of this shrine along the river Rushikulya (also called the Rushikalyani Saraswati and known as the elder sister of the Ganges in the Vedas) enhanced its religious and cultural significance.

Before the Mahabharat war Lord Krishna had advised Arjuna to offer prayer for victory to Goddess Bhadrakali. Bhadrakali is originated from Devi Sati's limb and is one of the sacred Shaktipeeths. It is therefore understood that all these Shaktipeeths were existed 6000 years ago. The famous Shaktipeeths of Bimala, Tara-Tarini, Dakshina Kalika and Kamakshi originated from the limbs of the divine corpse of Devi Sati. Sacred Texts like the Shiva Purana, the Kalika Purana, and the Devi Bhagavat attest this fact.

We travelled to Brahmapur by Madras Mail and reached in the morning next day. From Brahmapur rail station we travelled to our Gopalpur hotel by auto.

When we reached the hotel it was drizzling, which soon became a shower. So we prefer to stay indoors. There was a small portico attached to our room from where the sea could be seen very clearly. We both sat there and keep enjoying the view of the Bay of Bengal. We spent much of time by this way. In the afternoon we visited the famous Gopalpur sea beach and had nice times.

In the night we planned our sight-seeing trip for next day. Next morning vehicle reported on time. We started early. Leaving Brahmapur we travelled for about an hour. Soon our car left the plain land and took the Ghat road to manoeuvre a height of about 700 ft of the Kumari Hills (also called Purnagiri) to reach the hill top covering a total distance of about 45 km. Driver parked the car at the taxi stand. We walked down the temple complex. Soon we were before the Tara Tarini Shrine. We had a magnificent view of the meandering Rushikulya River below the hill. From the outside we took a close up shot of the temple.

There was not much rush in the temple inside. We climbed up a few stairs and reached the assembly hall and stood in the small queue of the worshippers. Soon we reached before the Garbhagriha (the sanctum sanctorum). When our turn came to see the image of the Goddess my wife handed over the flowers and the puja offerings to the Priest. We closed our eyes for a while and offered our prayer. The priest returned the puja Pushp and Prasad to us and blessed us. We stood for a while before the Goddess and prayed for the well being of all. Then we came out of the temple. It was drizzling outside.

On the courtyard outside we found the temple place where Yajna used to be held. There was also a place showing the practice of offerings of animals sacrifice. We took a round on the temple premises. There were four small temple like structures in the four corner of the premises. Incidentally they were closed. From the top of the hill we could see the sacred Rusikulya river distinctly. The Rushikulya River is one of the major rivers in the state of Odisha and covers entire catchment area in the districts of Kandhamal and Ganjam of Odisha. The Rushikulya originates at an elevation of about 1000 metres from Daringbadi hills of the Eastern Ghats range.

We found the historically famous Jaugada rock edict of Emperor Ashoka near the Shrine. The pious river Rushikulya has been described in Rig Veda as 'Gangayah Jyestha Bhagini' (the elder sister of the Ganga). The Hindu temple of the twin Goddess, Architecture of the temple and natural beauty surrounding the hill are main attraction of this place.

Adi Shakti goddesses Tara Tarini have been regarded as the presiding deity (Ista-Devi) (**Fig 4**). The goddesses Tara and Tarini are represented by two ancient stone statues decorated with gold and silver ornaments. Two stones anthropomorphized by the addition of gold and silver ornaments and shaped to be seen as human faces are the main shrine of this temple which represents the goddesses Tara and Tarini (**Fig 5**). In between them are two fully celebrated and beautiful brass heads as their Chalanti Pratima or their Living Image. We spent sometimes on the temple premises. The birds eye view of the surroundings of the hill below really enthralled us. We had a few beautiful moments there.

It is known from the available sources that till 17th century this place was out of the sight of the common man. According to a folk story once Maa Tara Tarini appeared as two sisters in the house of Shri Basu Praharaj, a learned Brahmin of Kharida Vira Jagannathpur village in the Ganjam district. He was a great devotee of the Mother Goddess Adi Shakti. He was child less. Two sisters stayed with the priest happily for some years. One day they disappeared suddenly from the house of Basu Praharaj. According to the account of the villagers the sisters travelled up to the Tarini Parvat/Ratnagiri and disappeared there. Basu Praharaj searched these girls but did not find their tracings. His heart broke down with grief and pain. On that night he had a dream where the Tara and Tarini informed Basu Praharaj that they were not his daughters; they are the Adi Shakti, Tara and Tarini. The Goddess ordered Basu to come out of the grief and instead he should conduct with full devotion renovation of the temple on the hilltop of Tarini Parvat and establish the deities there according to the Vedic tradition.

After that divine direction Basu discovered the tracings of the ancient most presence of Adi Shakti Tara Tarini on the sacred hilltop. He immediately took steps to reconstruct the temple and the shrine. Since that time for its magnetism and sanctity this Sthana Peetha (Breast Shrine) of Devi Sati, became a centre of faith and reverence for countless people. The abode of Goddess Adi Shakti attracted the people who were in search of peace, tranquility, guidance and spiritual energy. Its fame spread like wild fire to become one of the popular religious destinations for millions of devotees.

This region of Odisha has a unique history. Kalinga capital Sampa was hardly 7 km from this Tara Tarini Hills shrine. So, scholars believed that Tara Tarini was worshiped as the principal deity (Ista-Devi) of the mighty Kalinga Empire. About 2300 years ago Mauryan Emperor Ashoka occupied this area defeating the Kalinga Empire. Ashoka strengthened the grip of Buddhists in this part of India and made this place a famous centre of Buddhism. The region of Ganjam near the bank of river Rushikulya was an active Buddhist site as seen from the Special Rock Edicts of Ashoka found at Jaugada at a distance of 4 km from Tara-Tarini Hill Shrine. The name Tara, an important deity of Mahayana Buddhist Pantheon, is suggestive of Buddhist influence. Also an image of Buddha in meditation, present inside the sanctum sanctorum of the temple lends credence to the claim of this site as an ancient centre of the Buddhist Shakta cult.

Although in the initial days, the Buddhists didn't believe in the worship of Goddesses or in Pratimapuja (Idol Worship). But, the ecclesiastical texts of Mahayana's reveal that from 1st century AD after the fall of Kalinga, for the first time the Mahayana Buddhists accepted the worship of Mother Goddess 'Tara'. So there was seldom any doubt that the Buddhists had learned the 'Tara' Puja concept from this shrine. The Buddha Tantrik texts, texts of Vajrajani sect and Hindu Tantrik texts all agreed with these facts. Scholars believe that in the early days the Buddhists worshiped Taratarini of the Hindu Tantrik sect as Buddha Tara. Later on they included 'Tara' as the Tantrik deity or spouse of bodhisattva Avalokiteshvara in their belief system. Gradually this 'Tara' worship spread to different parts of the world.

The maritime history of Kalinga suggests that besides the Buddhist Tantrics, the Sadhakas, merchants and seamen before launching their sea voyage from the great sea ports like Dantapura (Gopalpur), Pallur near Chilika Lake, Kalingapatna and river Rushikulya used to worship Tara. All these major sea ports of the ancient world were very near to the Tara Tarini hill shrine.

We spent about an hour on the hill top and thoroughly soaked with the deep blessing of Goddess Adi Shakti. Then we drew an end to our stay and proceeded for next sightseeing.

Vishalakshi

That was the time when we were living in Kanpur. We visited the Vishveshwar Mahadev Jyotirling Shrine at Varanasi. After paying our reverence and offering our prayers to Lord Shiva at the Great Shrine we came out. That was quite an enriching experience both morally and physically.

We exited from the temple through the gate yielding to the narrow Kashi Vishwanath lane. We walked along the lane for a while for a distance of about 50 meters from the Jyotirling Shrine. We reached in front of a beautiful gate on our left standing just on the side of the lane.

We would have missed the gate had the gopuram (ornamented tower) depicting the Gajalakshmi murti in white marble not attracted our notice. The gate appeared to be just like a gate of any house but for the flanking by two stony lions welcoming the pilgrim. We were told this small house like building as the Goddess Vishalakshi Temple.

This temple is also known as Vishalakshi Gauri Temple. This is one of the eighteen Maha-Shakti Peeths, the most Holy Shrine devoted to the Hindu Divine Mother, Adi Shakti. Hindus believe the ear ring or the eyes of the Goddess Sati fell here from her half-burnt corpse when Vishnu's Sudarshan Chakra severed her corpse into multiple pieces. But as it is said there exist some difference about the body part Devi Sati of that fell here in Varanasi.

After removing our footwear we entered the temple. Feet felt the coolness of the black and white marble tiles, arranged like a chess board. We were to circumambulate the main shrine which housed the goddess' sacred image. The inner periphery of the temple is essentially a concrete wall. There was an area protruding like a shelf and displaying an assortment of Shiva lingams, with an accompanying Nandi, Nagas (divine serpents) and a Ganesh sculpture. There was also a marble statue of Adi Shankaracharya. On the right side of the temple was an adjacent room. It contains two gated areas housing a sculpted horse and an alternative image of the goddess Vishalakshi. There is a small shrine dedicated to Shiva in the form of a large lingam. Then we saw an altar upon which rests nine statues: Surya (Sun), Chandra (Moon), Mangala (Mars), Budha (Mercury), Brihaspati (Jupiter), Shukra (Venus), Shani (Saturn), Rahu (Ascending/North lunar node) and Ketu (Descending/South lunar node).

Then we reached the portico, most ornamented area directly in front of the main Shrine. Four painted pillars with sculpture of floral designs, Yantras and figures covered it. The ceiling over it produced a canopy-like effect. Finally we reached the main shrine of the Goddess Vishalakshi. We found that the sanctum sanctorum (Garbhagriha) contained a very ornate marble shrine. It contains an even smaller shrine housing the image. The original ancient murti and its accompanying shrine were placed in the larger shrine. It appeared that the current structure was quite literally built up around the old one.

The temple premise was not much crowded. It was relatively easy for us to find the beautiful image of the goddess Vishalakshi. The image is carved from a solid piece of polished black stone. Her upraised right arm bears a lotus in its hand, while the palm of her left, downturned hand is empty and facing away. She gazes directly forward. Interestingly her darshan can easily be obtained from the street itself when the front doors are open.

Then we were told that this stone sculpture was not the original representation of Vishalakshi. It was in fact carved from stone in 1971 when the temple was renovated. The priest was kind enough to guide us and asked to look at the Goddess from the side. Surprisingly we found another, smaller murti adorned with flowers directly behind the main image. We were told that this was the original image of Vishalakshi as she has been worshiped for countless years, since very ancient time. This black stone image of the goddess is swayambhu, or self-formed. This Vishalakshi original image was not made with human hands, but is a natural rock formation came from the earth that resembles a feminine form and has come to be worshiped as a self-manifested image of the goddess Vishalakshi (**Fig 6**).

According to the medieval Tantrik scripture, the Mahapithanirupana this is not the location where the Goddess Sati's earring had fallen. That location is said to be Manikarnika Kund. But Vishalakshi temple is named as Varanasi's presiding Shaktipeeth goddess as the Image there is believed to be self-formed or swayambhu. Some sources also believe that one of Goddess's eyes had fallen at this place. Nevertheless we decided to visit the Manikarnika Kund also. It was close by. Manikarnika Kund is an ancient sacred well.

Hindus believe that the followers of Shaktism pursue their Tantric work for seeking extraordinary power in the Shakti Peeths. One such Tantrik work Rudrayamala, composed before 1052 CE, mentions 10 principal Shakti Peethas, which includes Varanasi as the fifth one. Another work the Kularnava Tantra mentions this as the sixth of the 18 Peeths. The Ashtadashapitha (18 Peethas) ascribed to Adi Shankaracharya enumerates 18 names which included the Vishalakshi temple in Varanasi as the fifth Peetha. In the Kubjika Tantra, Varanasi is third among 42 names. Vishalakshi of Varanasi is mentioned as first of 108 Shakti Pithas in the list in the Devi Bhagavata Purana. The face of Sati is described to have fallen here. This is the only instance where a body part is related to the Shakti Peeth in the text. The Devi Gita within the same text gives a long list of Peeths, where Vishalakshi is mentioned as dwelling in Avimukta (present day Varanasi). The Pithanirnaya or Mahapithanirupana section from the Tantrachudamani listed Manikarnika at Varanasi with Vishalakshi as the presiding goddess comes in at number 23 out of 51 Peeths. A kundala (earring) is the anga-pratyanga and Kala-Bhairava is the consort.

The Vishalakshi temple is also popularly known as Annapurna Temple, the goddess of food. Consort of Shiva Parvati is given the epithet Vishalakshi, the "wide-eyed" and has made this her most famous temple in Varanasi where Goddess herself is the patron of the wellbeing of human. The *Skanda Purana* narrates the tale of the Sage Vyasa. He cursed Varanasi, as no one in the city offered him food. Finally, Vishalakshi appears in the form of a housewife and grants food to Vyasa. There Goddess Vishalakshi took the role of Goddess Annapurna, who offered food to her husband Shiva. The legend has it: Once Shiva told Parvati that food and other materials around does not mean anything and have no value. Goddess Parvati was sad to listen. She then stopped food production and all other materialistic items around. As a result very soon the universe was on the brink of food crisis and living beings started getting vanished. Shiva realised the mistakes and went to Parvati for food as he knew his hunger could only be satiated by her food. Goddess Parvati took her Annapurna form with golden pot and ladle and did Anna Dan with her own hand to Lord Shiva at Varanasi. Shiva gratified by Annapurna's food, established her temple at Varanasi where she was the presiding goddess. Thus the Goddess Vishalakshi has been identified with Goddess Annapurna as one since ancient times.

With high faith and belief people worship the Goddess Annapurna or the Maa Vishalakshi. They chant songs in her favour and offer puja to this most powerful and kind hearted Devi Shakti with the idea in turn that they would be blessed by the Goddess. We paid our reverence to Goddess Annapurna or Vishalakshi and came out of the Shrine shortly after. Although our visits were hectic but we enjoyed them as they opened before us many important information

The legend has it. Goddess Parvati during her bathing in this sacred tank once left behind one of her ornaments, a jeweled earring, or Manikarni. It seems therefore that the medieval Tantrik writers developed the idea that the Goddess Sati's earring fell to the earth at the site of Manikarnika Kund. That was how the Shakta worshippers started actively worshipping the Goddess Vishalakshi as Manikarni Devi. Mythologically speaking, the self-formed, original murti of the goddess corresponds directly with the earring of Sati which fell to earth countless aeons ago. While the ancient textual sources claim Manikarnika to be the location of the dropped earring, modern local knowledge points to the Vishalakshi Mandir as Varanasi's Shaktipeeth. The Brahmins agree with this idea. This Shaktipeeth is said to be one of the Ashthadasha Shaktipeeths.

Jwalaji

We had settled down in Kolkata after my superannuation from service. Earlier we had visited Himachal Pradesh three times prior to this visit and covered Shimla, Narkanda, Manali, Chamba, Bharmour, Dharamshala, Dalhousie and a few more places. Those were times of our prime youth. This time we planned to visit Himachal Pradesh once again but with a different purpose. That was mostly for spiritual persuasion at our older age.

Himachal Pradesh is said to the abode of Goddess Durga. There are seven Hindu pilgrimage sites in Himachal Pradesh dedicated to the different incarnations of Goddess Durga – Mata Chamunda Devi (Kangra), Mata Jwalaji (Kangra), Maa Kangra Devi (Kangra), Maa Chintpurni Devi / Mata Chhinnamastika Dham (outer Kangra), Mata Naina Devi (Bilaspur), Mata Mansa Devi (Hasampur) and Mata Kalika Devi (close to Shimla).

Our destination this time was Kangra and Palampur. Kangra is a district of Himachal Pradesh and is situated on the west-south part of the state. Here the mighty Himalaya gradually loses heights while Shivalik range starts. Mighty Beas River flows through the Kangra Valley. Beautiful Dhauladar mountain range and endless tea plantations of Palampur forms the northern backdrop of the town. Kangra has been described in the Holy Hindu texts as the Home of Hindu Gods and Goddesses. We were particularly interested to bow before Goddess Adi Shakti in her two important abodes or Shaktipeeths located in the region.

We travelled from Howrah by Himgiri Express and got down at Pathankot Cantt. Right from the station we hired a taxi and reached Kangra. At Kangra we got down at our reserved hotel and straightway completed checked in. After getting refreshed we checked with the travel desk. We fixed next day's sightseeing trip which included visit to temples of Chintpurni Devi, Jwalaji Devi and Brajeshwari Devi besides others in between. Hotel manager informed that Jwalaji temple was close to our hotel. So we could not resist. In the evening we walked down to the temple. Luckily it was the time of her Sandhya Aarti which we witnessed in an ambiance of great reverence.

Next morning we got up early. After taking bath and getting freshen up we started for Jwalaji Devi darshan. As we knew the route it was easy and quick. We took entry ticket and stood in the moderately long queue. The temple is situated at the bottom edge of the Shivalik mountain ridge called Kali Dhar in the Kangra district. We gradually moved ahead through the well fenced long marbled path.

The temple style is typical of Jwala Ji shrines, four cornered built in Mandap style with dome on the top. The interior consists of a square central pit of hollowed rock stone. Our turn came after some times. We were in front of the temple. We noticed inside carefully and found a bright flame is burning endlessly (**Fig 7**). It is felt as if natural gas is escaping through a crack in the hollowed rock wall and was burning endlessly. It is said Sati's tongue fell at Jwalaji (at elevation 610 m) and the goddess is manifested as tiny flames that burn flawless blue through the fissures in the rock. Hence this abode of Goddess Adi Shakti is dedicated to her in the name as Devi Jwalaji. It is believed to be one of the most ancient temples whose mention is found in the Mahabharata and other texts. We stood for a while inside the natural cave and saw the eternal flames burning flawlessly. Some say there are nine flames representing nine Durgas. Devi Jwalaji or also called Maa Jwala Mukhi is known to be family Goddess or Kuladevi of Lakhanpal's, Thakurs, Gujrals and Bhatia's of the region. The temple was in the jurisdiction of Firuz Shah Tughlaq when the Delhi Sultanate overran the Kangra. There are many legends float in the air. One of the legends has it. As per the legend It is said that centuries ago, a cowherd found that one of his cows was always without milk. He followed the cows to find out the cause. He saw a girl coming out of the forest and then she drank the cow's milk. She then disappeared in a flash of light. The Cowherd went to the King Bhumi Chand of Kangra and told him the story. The King was aware of the legend that Sati's tongue had fallen in this area. He tried to find the sacred spot but without success.

Some years later, the cowherd went to the King to report that he had seen a flame burning in the mountains. The King found the spot and saw the flame. He immediately termed it as the Holi flame and took control of the place. King was a great devotee of goddess Durga. When grief stricken Shiva was engaged in his Tandav Nritya with burnt corpse of Sati on his shoulder after her self-immolation, Vishnu had to cut her body by his Devine disc "Sudarshan Chakra". Out of the 51 body parts, Sati's tongue fell at this spot. At this place goddess Adi Shakti (who incarnated as Sati) is manifested as tiny flames that burn flawless blue through fissures in the age old rock. This sacred place has become one of the most revered Shaktipeeths. Devi Sati is worshipped here as Mata Jwalaji. King Raja Bhumi Chand built a temple there and arranged for priests to engage in regular worship. It is believed that the Pandavas came later and renovated the temple.

Jwalaji or Jwalamukhi temple as it is addressed sometimes has been a pilgrimage centre for many years. The Mughal Emperor Akbar once tried to extinguish the flames by covering them with an iron disk and even channeling water to them. But the flames blasted all these efforts. Akbar then presented a golden parasol (chattar) at the shrine. However, his cynicism at the power of Devi caused the gold to debase into another metal which is still unknown to the world. Consequent to this incident Akbar's belief in the deity was all the more strengthened.

It is a rare Hindu temple where the physical manifestation of Goddess is a flame. There are always 7 or 9 flames burning all the times. Government backed surveys have not been able to conclusively prove presence of gas which was thought to power the flame. Furthermore natural gas ascending levels of over 2000 feet above sea level where the temple is located – that is unheard of. Hence the actual source of energy powering the flame has remained a mystery.

After paying our reverence to Goddess Jwalaji we came out and stood in the temple courtyard. Mata Jwalaji Temple is one of the Ashthadasha Shaktipeeths. We look around and took a few photographs of the beautiful surroundings. We returned to hotel and completed our breakfast.

Chintpurni

As we completed our breakfast the taxi also reported. Shortly thereafter we started our journey for visiting Chintpurni temple, the other Shaktipeeth in this part of Himachal Pradesh.

We drove through the Kangra Una road. After driving for about an hour our taxi took a right hand cut towards the southernly direction. Soon after we reached a place called Bharwal located in Amb tehsil in Una district. The temple dedicated to Mata Chintpurni Devi is located in Bharwal. Mata Chintpurni Devi is also known as Mata Chhinnamastika Devi. After a point on this road no vehicle was allowed to go. We walked up the remaining way which was in upward gradient. As we were climbing up along the hilly road the picturesque surroundings of the temple was opening up before us.

The temple is situated at an altitude of 940 meters. Soon we reached the temple complex. We bought puja articles and the offerings for the Goddess from the roadside shops situated nearby. Very soon we joined the devotees in the moderately long queue. The temple is situated in the mountain zone created by the western end of the Himalaya on one side and one of highest peaks of the Sola Singhi range of the Shivalik Mountain rising on the other.

Soon our turn came and we were before the temple. Simple structure of the temple contains an entry hall and the main temple having the Garbh Griha. We found the goddess Chintpurni Devi depicted without her head in a pindi form (round stone) sitting on the round lotus petal (**Fig 9**). Hindus believe Sati's feet fell at this place at an altitude of over 900 m when Lord Vishnu's Sudarshan Chakra was severing the half burnt corpse of Sati into many parts.

Sati's self-immolation had convinced Hindus about Devi Sati's selfless interest and for betterment of the mankind against oppressions and wrong doings. This aspect of Devi Sati has made Hindus considering this Shaktipeeth to be dedicated to Mata Chhinnamasta Devi. The compassionate Mata Chhinnamasta Devi always fulfils the desire of the oppressed mankind. Mata Chhinnamasta is the self-sacrifice divine avatar of Devi Parvati which resembles the self-sacrifice of Devi Sati. Thus Chintpurni Shaktipeeth also came to be known as Mata Chhinnamasta Devi temple. Hindu devotees have been flocking the revered shrine Chintpurni Shaktipeeth for centuries to worship at the lotus feet of Mata Chhinnamastika Devi.

We also noticed that the inside wall of the temple had the stone cut idol of Mata Chhinnamasta Devi depicting her pose where Devi had cut her head (**Fig 8**)which is held in one hand while the other holding the scimitar. Blood was coming out profusely in many directions one of which was getting into the mouth of her cut head; others were being falling into the mouths of her two hungry associates.

The legend has it this way. Once the Gods and Goddesses were harassed and threatened by the two ferocious demons Shumbha and Nishumbha. Devi Parvati pursuing Shakti bestowed herself with additional powers and took a new divine avatar. She then proceeded with her two associates Dakini and Varini (also known as Jaya and Vijaya) to fight the demons and finally killed them.

After killing them Devi Mata Parvati with Her aides went to take a bath in the Mandakini River. After the dip in the river Mata Parvati regained her normalcy. She was feeling happy and excited. Her complexion darkened and the feeling of love completely took over. Her associates on the other hand were hungry after bath and asked Parvati to give them some food. Parvati requested them to wait and said that she would feed them after a while and began walking.

After some time, Jaya and Vijaya once again appealed to Maa Parvati by praising her as the Mother of the Universe. They prayed once again to feed them as they were her children. Parvati advised them to wait till they reach home. But two associates could not wait any longer and demanded that their hunger be satisfied immediately. The compassionate Mata Parvati laughed and with her finger nail cut her own head. Immediately, blood spurted in three directions. Jaya and Vijaya drank the blood from two directions and the Goddess herself drank the blood from the third.

Since Mata Parvati cut her own head, this avatar of her become known as Devi Chinnamasta. Devi Parvati took this avatar to fulfil the desires of her children, her devotees. This event complemented the Shaktipeeth, the abode of Devi Sati at the village Chintpurni in the Una district. Thus the Shaktipeeth shrine also came to be known as Mata Chintpurni. It is also believed by Hindus that the Chintpurni ("She who fulfills one's wishes") Chhinnamasta is one of the Ashthadasha Shaktipeeths (abode of Devi Sati), where the goddess Sati's forehead (*mastaka*) fell. Here, Chhinnamasta is interpreted as the severed-headed one as well as the fore headed-one. The central icon is thus seen as a *pindi*, an abstract form of Devi. While householders worship the goddess as a form of the goddess Durga, ascetic sadhus view her as the Tantric severed-headed goddess.

The legend associated with the temple has it that there was a priest Bhai Mai Das in the Chintpurni village. He was an ardent devotee of Goddess Durga. Once, the Goddess came in his dream and asked him to build a temple at this place. Following the instruction, the temple was built in Chhaproh village. Till date, his descendants perform the worship of Devi Chintpurni.

Shortly after we completed our darshan, we came out of the temple. We bought some sweet products from the shops nearby. Then we walked down the hilly path to reach our taxi and started back to Kangra town. We were told by the driver that the Brajeshwari Devi temple was closed. So we had to abandon our plan of visiting the third Shaktipeeth. We straightway returned to our hotel with a wonderful feeling of contentment.

Vindhyavasini

Mata Vindhyavasini is the benevolent Yogmaya aspect of Devi Amba or Durga. Her temple is located at Vindhyachal, 8 km away from Mirzapur on the banks of river Ganges, in Uttar Pradesh.

At the time of the birth of Krishna as 8th Child of Devaki-Vasudeva, Maha-Yogini Mahamaya had also taken birth at a child of Nanda-Yashoda. As per the instruction from God Vishnu, Vasudev had replaced Krishna with this girl child of Yashoda. When Kansa tried to kill this girl child she escaped upward from the hand of Kansa and turned into Devi Durga form. Kansa heard divine sermon from the sky saying, "Oh, Kansa, you fool, what will be the use of killing me? The Supreme Personality of Godhead, who has been your enemy from the very beginning and who will certainly kill you, has already taken His birth somewhere else. Therefore, do not unnecessarily kill other children". Saying this she vanished from the prison of Mathura. Thereafter, she chooses Vindhyachal Mountains to reside.

The goddess gets her name Vindhyavasini from Vindhya Mountain Range. The name Vindhyavasini literally means she who resides in Vindhya. It is believed Goddess Adi Shakti in her incarnation as Parvati created the hillock which is known as Vindhyachal. Goddess Parvati killed demon Mahishasura at this place where the present temple stand today. It is believed Vindhyachal is the place where Devi had chosen to reside after her birth. This is also considered as one of the Shaktipeeths where Devi Sati's toe had fallen.

The temple is one of the most revered Shakti Peethas of India. The Vindhyavasini Devi is also known popularly by name of Kajala Devi. Goddess Kali is adorned in the form of Vindhyavasini Devi. We were residing at Kanpur that time. From there in one Puja vacation we went to Varanasi on a leisure trip. From Varanasi on a day sightseeing trip we visited the Vindhyachal Dham for paying our reverence to Goddess Vindhyavasini.

Maa Vindhyavasini temple is in Mirzapur district surrounded by many hills all around. We started on a hired taxi early in the morning from Varanasi. Distance between Varanasi and Maa Vindhyavasini the temple is 63 km. Taxi took the National Highway 2 and driving for about an hour it took turn southward at Aurai a place between Allahabad and Varanasi. After crossing Holy River Ganga, through Shastri Bridge taxi took the State Highway no. 5. The road condition was poor. It took more than an hour to cover 19 km distance. We finally reached the foothills of Vindhyachal. Maa Vindhyavasini temple was on a hill. So our car took us to the top of the hills and from there we walked down to reach the temple complex. We have to climb a few stairs to reach the temple gate. My wife bought flowers and puja offerings from the nearby flower shop. We then entered temple hall after climbing a few more stairs. There was no system of any queue for pilgrims. So there was total chaos. In the mille we got separated. My wife got pushed ahead by the moving crowd. Possibly my wife could manage to slip through and went ahead in the flow of the milieu. She could alone offer our prayer before the Goddess Vindhyavasini (**Fig 10**). In the unprecedented chaos created by the unorganized pilgrim all rushing at the same time I was forced to fall back. As a result I could not proceed ahead and preferred to come back. Then I stood at the Garbhagriha exit door to receive my wife.

My wife was so terrified in my absence among the crowd that she came out weeping. I tried to console her and narrated the story how we were separated in the mille. This was our experience of this great Shaktipeeth. We had been to so many temples before this. But no where we found such maddening and indiscipline crowd more like hooligans than worshippers. There was absolutely no management of the crowds. On the contrary it was found that the local pandas intentionally created this chaos. The Temple is never short of crowd and bustle.

Nevertheless with our clean heart and mind we offered our reverence to the Goddess and came back with happy feelings. Vindhyachal is the home of Devi Adi Shakti where she stayed much of her time in her incarnation as Parvati or Durga. Here the Deity of the Goddess appeared showing her Mukhmandal duly ornamented and garlanded with many demon-heads. Her appearance sends the message to her worshipper about her great strength and aggressiveness towards evil power and wrong doings.

Gadkalika

We had just completed our darshan to Mahakaleswar Mahadev at Ujjain. Then our taxi driver cum guide informed us about the presence of a Shakti Peeth situated nearby. But he was not sure about the exact location. After contacting a nearby local shopkeeper he came to know about the location of the temple.

It is a small temple on the outskirts of Ujjain about 2 km from the city. After travelling for about half an hour we could leave the town behind. Soon we were in the midst of the lush green landscape of the countryside. The place is known as Gad Village. After a few minutes we realised that we had reached near the temple. Commonly known as the Kalika Devi temple, it was also revered as the Gadkalika Temple as per the name of the village. The beautifully built temple was an ancient one. The temple is said to have remodeled in the 7th century AD by Emperor Harshavardhan. Subsequently it was believed to have been renovated during the Paramara period. The present form of the temple was given in the modern times by the erstwhile Gwalior State.

Situated near the Bharathihari cave and on the bank of the river Shipra Kalika Devi shrine is considered by the Hindus as very powerful. The legend goes like this. Great poet Kalidasa was originally uneducated, but with his great devotion to the goddess Kalika, he acquired unparalleled literary skills. Devi Goddess was pleased with Kalidasa's devotion and wrote beejakshar on the tongue of Kalidasa and made him a great poet.

The crowd was not much. We saw a statue of a lion at the entrance which is the vehicle of the Goddess. We crossed the statue and entered the temple premises. My wife had bought Puja basket containing flowers, fruits

and other cosmetic items for the Goddess Kalika which included red Chunri, bangles, kumkum, perfumed stick, rice and so on. We entered through the Mandap which had many pillars to reach the Puja Offer room from where we looked at the Garbhagriha. The presiding Deity of the Shrine Devi Kalika was seen beautifully decorated with ornaments (**Fig 11**).

We offered our prayer to the Goddess Gadkalika with due reverence. We stood before the Devi Mata for sometimes dipping in the venerable atmosphere. We were told that Kumkum Archana was done there. Many people offer bangles, rice and other things for their wellbeing and for better education for their children. We saw a big lamp installed in the premises which also housed the temple of Ganesh and Hanuman. We were overwhelmed with the serenity and tranquility of the temple premises.

Devi Gadkalika Shrine is one of 18 Maha Shaktipeeths (Ashthadasha Shaktipeeths). It is believed that the Upper Lip of Sati Devi had fallen here when Vishnu's Sudarshan Chakra severed the corpse of Devi Sati being carried on his shoulder by Shiva during his Tandav Nritya.

The Goddess Gadkalika idol is said to be even older than the temple itself which is believed to be older than the Mahabharata period.

We were told that there was a very famous cave named Bharthrihari situated close by. These caves are situated just above the bank of the Shipra River. According to popular tradition, this is the spot where the great Sanskrit Poet Bharthrihari, lived and meditated after renouncing worldly life. He is said to have been the step brother of King Vikramaditya. He is believed to have written his famous works, Shringarshatak, Vairagyashatak, and Nitishatak while staying here.

The calm and peaceful surrounding of the Shrine left an unforgettable imprint on our mind which we remember till date.

Bhramarambha Devi

It was our second trip to south India that we made from Kolkata. We were settled down nicely in Kolkata after retirement. One morning I was searching the location of a place Srisailam on the Railway map. On her question "Why Srisailam?" I clarified my wife that it was the place where a Shiva Jyotirlinga is situated. Promptly concurred by both we decided to visit the Mallikarjuna Mahadev Jyotirling Shrine at Srisailam. This would be our tenth Jyotirlinga. Incidentally this Shrine is accompanied with the great Shaktipeeth named Goddess Bhramarambha Devi temple as well. So we will have two famous pilgrimages in one trip.

We travelled by SSPN Express from Howrah and got down at Markapur Road station. This is situated on the Nallapadu – Nandyal section of Guntur railway division of the South Central Railway zone. From there we took an auto and reached the Markapur Bus stand. After checking with the ticket office we got into the right bus for Srisailam. The distance between Markapur town and Srisailam is 81 km. The hilly track of about 46 km of this distance was through Nallamala Forest. This forest is full of Kadali and Bilva trees, covering both sides of the road. We travelled through the curvy road and partly untouched tribal terrain for almost 3 hrs. Finally we reached Srisailam in the evening and checked in AP Tourism Resort.

We took hot water bath, which removed our day long exhaustion and refreshened completely. In the night we went out for dinner.

We walked down the lane amidst calmness and freshness. We came across the Jyotirlinga Shrine of Mallikarjuna Mahadev temple situated very close to our hotel. We had our dinner in one of the restaurants in downtown and return to hotel by 9:30 pm.

Next morning we woke up early and reached the Temple premises. After purchasing the necessary ticket we entered the temple compound and stood in the required Queue.

The existing main temple is a huge complex consisting of separate temples of Mallikarjuna Mahadev and Devi Bhramaramba, several Sub Shrines, Pillared Halls, Mandapas, Springs etc. After completing our Darshan of Mallikarjuna Mahadev we came out and then stood in another line in front of the second temple. This line led us to the Shrine of Mata Bhramaramba Devi temple.

The temple is the seat of Mahakali in the form of Bhramaramba. The most appealing feature of this temple is that any one of any cast or creed can touch the deity and worship here. This Shrine is considered as the abode of Goddess Adi Shakthi (in her incarnation of Devi Sati). Here Devi Sati's *Greeva* (neck) is believed to have fallen when her corpse was severed by the Divine Disc of Vishnu.

The queue was not very long and soon we entered the Garbhagriha and stood before the Goddess. Goddess Brhamarambika is the consort of Mallikarjuna Swamy, a manifestation of Shiva. In this temple, goddess is worshiped in the form of Shakti. The idol of the Goddess has eight arms and is wearing a silk sari. Inside the Garbha Griha of the temple, there is an idol of Lopamudra, wife of sage Agastya. There is a Sri-Yantra in front of Garbha-Griha. There are many legends associated with the Bhramaramba Devi Temple. Once there was a demon named Arunasura. He was an ardent devotee of Brahmadev. Pleased with his unwavering dedication, Brahmadev blessed him with the powers that he could not be killed by any two or four legged living being. After receiving the boon, Arunasura started causing problems to Devas and Saints. Because of his immense powers, Devas couldn't defeat him. Gods prayed to Goddess Durga and pleased her to protect them. Hearing the plea of the oppressed

Goddess Durga took the form of Bhramari or Brhamarambika and created thousands of six legged bees that killed the demon.

The word Bhramaramba means "Mother of Bees". Later Goddess stayed back in the form Brhamarambika in Srisailam. We are all aware of the evolution of the Shaktipeeths. The Shaktipeeths are these places where body parts of Sati were believed to have fallen. Hindus believe that the neck of Sati had fallen at Srisailam and constitute as one of the eighteen Maha Shaktipeeths.

We offered our prayer and obedience to the Goddess and completed our darshan of the Maha – Shaktipeeths (**Fig 12**). It is one of the Ashta-Dasha Shaktipeeths. We stood for a while with sincere reverence before we were forced to move ahead. We came out of the Holy Shrine, heart filled with peace and satisfaction.

We had a very thrilling feeling inside us, thinking that we could come to this far away place which is ordinarily considered as a difficult place to reach. We always remember with reverence but for Shiva and Goddess Adi Shakti this trip could not have been possible. We moved around the place for few hours and returned to hotel but not before buying the tasty laddoos from the temple outlet. We liked this small hilly hamlet and fell in love in just two days. We carry a sweet memory of the place of Srisailam or the Sri Parvat. The taste of the laddoos still lives on our taste bud and rekindles our memory.

Kiriteshwari

I recollect that was an event of my childhood. I was studying in class eight when my youngest maternal uncle (Chhotomama) visited our house at Berhampore. My Chhotomama expressed before my mother about his desire to visit Mata Kiriteshwari temple. He wanted me to accompany him. I immediately jumped to the idea and took mother's permission to accompany him.

We reached Lalbagh Ghat (located on the eastern bank of the river Bhagirathi) in the Murshidabad district by Riksha about 12 km from our house. From there we took the Pheri (Boat drive) to cross the Bhagirathi River and reached the other bank.

From there we walked down the village road. We soon bypassed the Lalbagh court road rail station. From there our destination Kireetkona village was about 3 km. We continued to walk through the village path. We crossed through a deep forest to reach near a temple like structure. That was the Mata Kiriteshwari temple.

A glance at the forest made us to believe that people often comes here to have picnics. The Nabagram-Lalbagh road has passed through the Kireetkona village. The place is near Dahapara and Dahapara rail station is also close by.

Kiriteshwari Temple is the oldest, holiest and a famous religious place of Murshidabad district. This is one of the 51 Shaktipeeths. Hindus believe that the "crown" or the kirit of Sati had fallen here. Here Devi is worshipped as Vimala (meaning 'pure') and Shiva as Sambarta. The Shaktipeeth is considered as an Upa-Peeth, as no limb or body part fell here, but only a portion of her ornament fell here. It is one among the handful of temples in Bengal where no deities but an auspicious black stone is worshipped.

The original old name of Kiriteshwari was Kireetkona. Kireet means the crown. Kireetkona or Kiriteshwari is mentioned in the Bhavishyapurana, a literature written in the medieval period.

It is also heard that the temple Kiriteshwari existed in the time of Shankaracharya and the Gupta age. The construction of the temple is more than 1000 years old and this place was considered to be the sleeping place of Mahamaya. Local people call this temple as "Mahishamardini". It is the oldest mark of Architecture in Kiriteshwari.

The 'Bangadhikaris' or Kanoongos of Dahapara made extensive provisions for the maintenance of the Temple. One of their ancestors Bhagavan Rai received the area of Kiriteshwari as jagir from Delhi Sultanate. The original Kireetkona Temple was destroyed in 1405 AD. The temple was subsequently reconstructed several times.

It is believed that around 1730 Raja Kirtichand (1702-1740) of Burdwan Raj rebuilt it for the first time. Then seeing that sacred temple overgrown with jungle and dilapidated Bangadhikaris Darpa Narayan renovated it during the 19th century. He also built several new temples around and excavated a tank close by, called the 'Kali Sagar'. Later Yogendranaryan Roy, the late king of Lalgola had renovated and taken care of the temple built by Darpanarayan Roy. We felt that the temple was relatively old but regular Pujas and up keeping had kept it in good condition. That day number of pilgrims was moderate. We could see the temple after some waiting.

The temple building was built in a rectangular construction with many pillars in all the sides. The roof top of the Garbh Griha was in the form of a tomb with a difference unlike the Muslim style. We entered the Garbh Griha soon. We found there was no deity as normally we are accustomed. Goddess Kiriteshwari is represented by a Red coloured stone which is worshipped by the devotees. The Red coloured stone is covered with a veil and is changed only on Asthami of each Durga Puja and given a sacred bath.

The sacred stone is topped with the Devi face which had a on its head. The Kirit or crown has been worshipped through ages. The crown, or the frontal bone, itself, which is called *guptapit*, is preserved in a pot covered with red silk and is rarely exposed to public view. At present, the headdress is preserved at nearby Rani Bhavani's Guptamath located opposite to the temple. There is a high altar on which a small altar is seen. Here the face of Maa Kiriteshwari is indexed. This is one of the most popular Shaktipeeths of the eastern India (**Fig 13**).

We both offered our reverence to the Goddess. My Uncle who is a very pious and truthful person sat there for a while. After sometimes I came out and walked around the temple compound. There were many temples of different deities in the temple complex. They were in different stages of decaying. Adjacent to the temple 'Bhairav' is situated in an unclean and filthy small temple, on the banks of the river Bhagirathi. The said temple remains locked for hours.

The temple of Kiriteshwari has had all along a great sanctity attached to it. Mir Jafar when in death-bed, under the advice of Maharaja Nanda Kumar took the Charanamrita of Kiriteshwari. Rani Bhavani's son, Raja Ram Krishna was a devout Shakta (a person who worships Shakti as the wife of Shiva). He conducted his meditations on a seat placed over five human skulls under a Bel tree. He was a frequent visitor at the shrine at Kiriteshwari. It is said that he had a canal excavated from Baranagore to that place in order that he might get there by boat.

Annual fair is held at Kiriteshwari since the time of Darpa Narayan. This fair attracts many pilgrims who bathe and offer prayers, as well as picnickers. The temple of Kiriteshwari was a favorite place of Raja Ram Krishna, the husband of Rani Bhavani. When Murshidabad was at its peak of glory as capital Kiriteshwari Devi was worshipped by hundreds of devotees every day.

Many legends are associated with this temple. One of such, a tradition of the mysteries of Kiriteshwari as handed down to posterity is narrated here. One day a bangle seller, fatigued with his morning errand, stepped down to drink water of the tank near the temple. On the step next to water he found a very young girl performing her ablutions. She prevailed upon him to sell her a pair of bangle. The man slided the rings into the tiny hands of the young girl and when he demanded the price she referred him to her father, the Shebait (caretaker) of the temple of Kiriteshwari. She also mentioned that the money was in a certain place in the house. The man went to the Shebait and asked for the price of the bangles which his daughter had purchased. The Shebait thought the man was a cheat for he had no daughter. The man indicated the place where the money was kept as told by the girl. When it was searched it was found that money was there, although it was never kept before. The Shebait still suspicious asked the man to show him where his daughter was. They came to the steps of the tank but there was no body in the vicinity. The man began to weep, being reprimanded by the Shebait as a cheat, when two beautiful hands radiant with the light of divinity and bedecked with the pair of new bangles jutted forth from the water in the middle of the deep tank and soon disappeared. Both the Shebait and the seller stupefied as they were at this miraculous appearance. Legends also cluster round *Tara*, daughter of Rani Bhavani and to this day stories are told of how she escaped the evil designs of Siraj-ud-Daulla through the help of a saint named Mastaram. On one occasion, when the Nawab came to seize her, he found her suffering from small-pox and retired discomfited. The small-pox, which had been miraculously caused by the saint, at once disappeared in the same miraculous fashion.

Mastaram lived at Sadekbagh on the opposite side of the Bhaglrathi and had the supernatural gift of being able to walk, or of being transported by invisible agency, across the stream. The akhra at Sadekbagh, which was founded in 1646, is known as the Akhra of Mahant Mastaram Aulia. It was known that a fair is held on each Tuesday and Saturday of the month of Poush (Mid-Dec to Mid-Jan) at the temple compound on the western bank of the river Bhagirathi.

Jayadurga

After offering our reverence to Baidyanath Mahadev at the Jyotirling Shrine at Deoghar we came out and stood at the temple courtyard. We found many small temples (later counted to be as many as twenty) dedicated to various Hindu Gods and Goddesses, located all around the square. This Shrine is one of the twelve Jyotirlings of Shiva.

We are told that opposite to Mahadev's temple stands the Jayadurga Shaktipeeth. Jayadurga Shaktipeeth is popularly known as Baidyanath Dham or Baba Dham. This is located in the same premises as that of the Baidyanath. Baidyanath is believed to stand here as Bhairav to protect his consort Sati's temple where Sati is worshipped as Devi Jayadurga. Hindus believe Sati's Heart has fallen here when her burnt body after her self-immolation at father Daksha's Yajna fire is severed into many parts by Vishnu's Sudarshan Chakra. This is why the Shaktipeeth is also known as Hardapeeth.

Temple of Mata Sati standing exactly opposite to the temple of Vaidyanath is connected by red colored silk threads in their tops (**Fig 14**). There is a belief that the couple who binds these two tops with the silk will have a happy family life by the blessings of Shiva and Parvathi. The temple has a base which we climbed up through a few stairs. Then we passed though a small passage to enter the Garbh Griha. The queue was moderate. We found two idols were standing on a square type rock stage. People were offering milk, honey and flowers to the Goddesses. Two idols are said to be of Goddess Sati and Mata Parvati respectively.

Hindus believe many Tantrics worshiped Jayadurga and got her blessings. Here Jaganmata is worshiped in two forms – the first one is of Tripura Sundari or Tripura Bhairavi and the second one is of Chinnamasta. Tripura-Sundari is worshiped with Ganesh as Rishi and Chinnamasta is worshiped with Ravanasura as Rishi.

As we reached close to the Idols we bowed before the Goddess Shakti and offered our reverence. Shortly after our prayer we came out of the Jayadurga temple. The Shakti Peeth is also known as Chitabhumi. It is said that Shiva performed the cremation of her heart at this place. Hence the place derived its name as Chitabhumi.

Baidyanath Shakti Peeth is an auspicious place where a person gets relieved from incurable diseases like leprosy. It is believed that the person, who visits this place, gets freedom from all sorts of disease and all kinds of sins. Bad or negative thoughts are removed from a person's brain. Individual gets a spiritual growth.

Legend has that in the beginning of the Universe Shiva manifested himself as a lingam of light at twelve different places under different names and Baidyanath was one of those twelve places. Sati worshipped the emblem in the form of a pandanus flower on the top of the lingam and dwelt for a long time in a grove close by in order to worship it. This place is called Ketakivana.

Matsya Purana narrates about the sanctity of the holy place where Shakti lives and frees people from diseases, i.e., Arogya Baidyanathitee. It signifies that Baidyanath cures people from incurable diseases with the help of Shakti, the destroyer of diseases.

Baidyanath Dham being one of the 51-Shakti Peeths, Goddess Sati is worshipped as Jayadurga (Victorious Durga) and Bhairav as

Baidyanath. The relevance of the Peethas is associated with Devi Bhagwat, Kubjika Tantra, Kalika Rahasyam, Mundmal Tantra and Rudrayamalam etc. Mention of these Tantras made this holy shrine as a popular Tantrik seat for Sadhakas. Famous scholar and Tantric Gopinath Kaviraj have mentioned Baidyanath Dham, as a seat of Tantric Sadhana.

We spent some more time and completed seeing other temples one by one. A sense of great joy and relieve ran though our mind and body making our darshan of Baidyanath Dham not only memorable but also spiritually satisfied. Temple of Goddess Jayadurga is one of the Ashthadasha Shaktipeeths.

We were driven by the pinch of hunger as we did not have breakfast. So we rushed to the hotel but not before buying some more sweets (pedas) again.

Bhagwati Amman

It was almost a year then. We were settled in our home at Kolkata. Then the opportunity came before us.

Indian Railway decided to run a Special Train on a 12-day South India trip in the memory of Vivekananda's 125th Birth Anniversary. We immediately grabbed the opportunity and bought the tickets for us. In this trip we covered Hyderabad, Mysore, Bangalore, Trivandrum, Kanyakumari, Rameswaram and Madurai. Trip had started from Howrah and ended at Howrah.

On the 9th day we reached at Kanyakumari in the mid-night. Trip management had arranged our stay at a hotel nearby. Next day morning we were on our own for sight-seeing. We were thrilled by the thoughts alone that we are at the southern tip of our county. It was a dream coming true for both of us.

Getting up in the early morning we finished our morning rituals. We then had breakfast by the stuff provided by the tour management. After taking a bit of tour guidance from the hotel staff we straight way proceeded to Vivekananda Memorial Rock on the Indian Ocean. It was life's one of the greatest desires fulfilled. We completed our visit in about three hour's time. We came back to the land and then had some quick fast foods.

We then proceeded on foot to visit the Goddess Bhagwati Amman temple, which happened to be located very close by. We had to deposit our articles before entering the temple.

The Bhagavathy Amman Temple is located in Cape Kanyakumari town in Tamil Nadu, at the southern tip of main land India, by the side of the confluence of the Bay of Bengal, the Arabian Sea, and the Indian Ocean.

The deity of the temple is Devi Kanya Kumari. She is goddess Parvati in the form of an adolescent girl child. Devi is also known as Shree Bala Bhadra or Shree Bala. She is popularly known as "Devi Shakti". She is also known by several other names, including *Kanya Devi* and *Devi Kumari*. She is also worshiped as Shree *Bhadrakali* by devotees. Sage Parashurama is said to have performed the consecration of the temple. The goddess is believed to be the one who removes rigidity of the mind; devotees usually feel the tears in their eyes or even inside their mind when they pray to the goddess in devotion and contemplation.

Kanyakumari Temple is one of the 51 Shaktipeeths. It is believed that the right shoulder and (back) spine area of Sati's corpse fell here creating the presence of Kundalini Shakti in the region. Some believe that the Bhadra Kali Temple within Kanya Kumari Temple is the Shakti Peeth. Mention of Devi Kanya Kumari was in Ramayana, Mahabharata, and the Sangam works Manimekalai, Puranaanooru and Narayan Upanishad, a Vaishnava Upanishad in the Taittiriya Samhita of Krishna Yajur Veda

The feminine aspects of the Supreme Being (in its manifested and un-manifested forms) are called as Prakriti, and the male aspects are called as Purusha. The Prakriti is addressed in different names as Adi-Parashakti, Bhadra, Shakti, Devi, Bhagavathi, Amman, Rajarajeshwari, and Shodashi. In all the material manifested aspects the Nature is classified as feminine. Nature is the Prakriti or Mother Goddess. The un-manifested forms Knowledge, Prosperity and Power are considered as feminine Prakriti, and it is source of energy for Creation, Sustain and Control, which is the male aspect (Purusha) of Par Brahmadev.

In Tantra, the worship of Prakriti is done in different methods: Dakshinachara (Right-Hand Path) (Sattvik rites), Vamachara (Left-Hand Path) (Rajas rites) and Madhyama (Mixed) (Tamas rites) in different temples. The name of Devi in temples during Sattvik or Dakshina rites is 'Shree Bhagavathy' and Rajas (left method) rites is called 'Maha Devi' similar to Maha Vidya.

The mythological story dates back to the prehistoric Tamil period. Bana, an Asura by birth was the ruler of his land. He was a very powerful king. He practiced tapasya and obtained a boon from Brahmadev that his death will only be by an adolescent young girl.

With this powerful boon, he became fearless and wreaked havoc on the entire world. He went on to conquer and oust Indra from his throne. He banished all the Devas from there. The Devas who were the personification of the basic natural elements, Agni (fire), Varuna (water), Vayu (air) went uncoordinated and havoc spread in the universe, because Indra (ether) was not able to administer and coordinate the Pancha Bhoota.

Goddess Adi Parashakti being the unbiased Prakriti can only bring order back. All the Gods prayed to her for help. Adi Shakti as Bhagavathy manifested herself in the Southern tip of the Aryavartha to kill Bana. As an adolescent girl, she had immense devotion towards Shiva. Shiva decided to marry her. All arrangements were made for the marriage. Shiva started the journey from Suchindrum for the marriage. The marriage Muhurta (auspicious time) was in the Brahmadev Muhurta early in the morning.

Sage Narada played his trick. He knew Bana could only be killed by a young girl and thus interrupted Shiva's marriage with Bhagavathy. So he made the sound of a cock sending wrong information that the Sun had already risen and the auspicious time passed. The marriage procession returned.

Devi waited for the auspicious time but in vain. Finally she thought that she had been snubbed. With unbearable insult, pain, grief, and anger she destroyed everything she saw. She threw away all the food and broke her bangles.

When she finally gained her composure she undertook continuous penance. A few years later Bana tried to lure and approach the goddess without realizing who she was. The infuriated Bhagavathy, who was the Bhadrakali herself, slaughtered Bana at once. Moments before his death Bana realized that the one before him was Devi Adi Shakti, the Almighty herself. He prayed her to absolve him of his sins. After killing Bana, Devi assumed her original form of Parvati and reunited with her husband Shiva. Bhagavathy maintained her divine presence in the place, in the Devi Kanyakumari Temple.

After depositing our articles viz., cameras, mobile, bags, etc we stood in the queue. It was a long queue. When we near the entry of the temple I was asked to take out all my top garments as it was the essential requirement. We stood before the Goddess Deity at quite a distance (**Fig 15**).

The presiding image is sported in standing posture with an Akshamala (prayer beads) in her hands. There is an image of a lion in her pedestal indicating that she is the form of Durga. There is a four-pillar hall in the temple, each of which gives out sounds of Veena (a string instrument), Mrudanga (a percussion instrument), flute and Jalatharanga (porcelain instrument). The deity stands in the sanctum as a young girl absorbed in her penance with a rosary in her right hand. It is said that the deity was installed by Parashurama. We stood before her for a while and offered our reverence.

Kanyakumari Temple is one of the 51 Shaktipeeths. It is believed that the back spine area of Sati's corpse fell here creating the presence of Kundalini Sakti in the region. The shrine is accessed through the Western door. The goddess is considered as Devi Kutyayani, one of the Nava Durga here. She is also considered as Bhadrakali by devotees while worshipping her.

Devi Kanyakumari is the goddess of virginity and penance. This temple is one of the Ashthadasha Shaktipeeths. It is a practice that people choose to receive the Diksha of Sanyasa from here in olden times. The rites and rituals of the temple are organized and classified according to Sankaracharya treatise.

The other attractions inside the temple are the Patala Ganga Theertham, Kalabhairava Shrine. Kalabhairava is a ferocious form of Shiva who annihilates everything, i.e. Kala or time itself. Each of the 51 Shakti Peetam has a Kalabhairava shrine within the temple meant for the protection of the temple. In the Kanyakumari temple Kalabhairava is known as 'Nimish' and the Shakti is 'Sarvani'.

In the Shakti Peetham of Suchindrum the Kalabhairava is 'Sanhar' and the Shakti is 'Narayani'. These are two Shaktipeeths out of the 51 Shaktipeeths. We also saw two shrines to Vijayasundari and Balasundari dedicated to the friends and playmates of the Goddess in her youthful form. There was also a Navaratri hall on the Shri Pada Para, the rock in the shape of Devi's foot. This is now famous as Vivekananda Para, where Vivekananda got enlightenment to dedicate his life as an active Sanyasi rather than the usual practice of being passive.

The Gayatri of Devi Kanyakumari is: "Katyayini dhimahi Kanyakumari dhimahi tanno durgiḥ prachodayat". Red Sarees and Ghee wick lamps are offered to the goddess by devotees. Devi Kanya Kumari is goddess Shree Bhagavathy in the form of an adolescent girl child. As directed by his Guru Sri Ramakrishna Paramhansa, Swami Vivekananda came here to seek Devi's blessing in December 1892, as Devi is the goddess of Sanyasa. It is in this location he decided to embark on the missionary work to a higher level of action rather than being passive like the usual Sanyasa.

In olden days it was believed that Devi Amman's Diamond nose ring shine used to show the way for ships to reach the destination. This aspect is still valid as witnessed the shinning nose ring.

This temple is almost 3000 year old and stands beside the ocean. It is one of the Ashthadasha Shaktipeeths. Kanyakumari is one of the few places in the world which leave indelible impressions on the memory of a visitor. Place of Kanyakumari combines both aspects of being a beautiful place and holiest pilgrim centers of the country. It is the Land's End of India, where one may stand on the shore and watch sun rise from the Bay of Bengal and sun set in the Arabian Sea.

Hundreds of tourists and pilgrims of every creed and conviction, visit the place to bathe in the holy waters of the ocean and to offer worship at the sacred shrine or to enjoy the superb scenic beauty of the place.

Before ending we would like to share an interesting fact. The Gandhi Smarak Mandir on the beach at Kanyakumari was erected as a memorial to the Father of the Nation. It is so constructed that the rays of the sun at noon on Gandhiji's birthday will fall on the pedestal, through a hole on there of just above it.

The magnificent memorial to Swami Vivekananda is built on one of the twin rocks at the confluence of the three seas. The entire memorial is of granite, with its main dome of 60 ft. high is similar to that of Sri Ramakrishna Temple at Belur. Below the dome, in the main hall, is installed the standing parivrajak posture. It is eight and half feet high and mounted on a four and half feet pedestal.

Adjoining the main hall is the Dhyana Mandapam where devotees can sit and meditate in a calm and serene atmosphere. A separate shrine, Shripada Mandapam, is also constructed over the foot print of the Goddess. Swamiji's statue is facing this Mandapam.

We returned from the temple after collecting our articles. Our visit to this temple is still vividly reflecting in our remembrance.

Suchindram

After completing our visit to the Devi Kanyakumari Bhagwati Amman temple in Kanyakumari, we took our lunch in a nearby hotel. By then it was 3 O'clock. Our train was to start at 9 pm. Seeing that we had sometimes in hand we decided to have a quick sightseeing at Kanyakumari town. We hired an auto and indulged in a trip in the unknown world.

Soon we were travelling on the national highway which links Kanyakumari with Nagarcoil on the way to Travancore. It appeared as if the road was cut out of the mountains of the Eastern Ghat range as we saw mountains on both sides of the road. On both the sides of the road we found lot of Palm trees standing in line as if saluting the tourists. After visiting a few places and travelling for about 40 mins, the driver cum guide finally took us to the temple known as Suchindram Temple. The temple is in the Suchindram town which is 11 km from Kanyakumari city centre and 7 km from Nagarcoil.

The seven storied beautiful white Gopuram, the entrance tower to this temple is visible from a distance (**Fig 16**). Standing upright majestically for a height of 134 feet it welcomes us. The face of the tower is covered with sculptures and statues from Hindu mythology. We got down at the auto parking space and walked up to the entrance gate. There is a covered area in front of the main entrance and the entrance itself is about 24 feet high with a beautifully carved door. On the left of the main entrance we found a very large wooden Chariot was standing. There is only one corridor running along the outer wall of the temple with many shrines and Mandapam located in a scattered manner in the inner area.

It is understood that this temple attracts both Vaishnavites and Saivites in large numbers. There are as many as thirty Shrines dedicated to various deities within the temple complex. These include the large Lingam in the sanctum; the idol of Vishnu in the adjacent shrine and a large idol of Hanuman at the Eastern end of the Northern corridor which also hold the remaining of the deities of the Hindu pantheon.

There are many legends available. One legend has it. Anasuya, the wife of Atri Maharishi was famous for her chastity and her devotion to her husband – An embodiment of a Hindu wife. She could perform miracles by sprinkling the 'Paatha Theertham' (water with which she washed her husband's feet) to bring rain to a parched earth or to transform objects to her desire. When this fact reaches the ears of the three Goddesses – Lakshmi, Saraswati and Parvati through Sage Narada, they wanted to test her chastity. They approached their husbands Brahmadev, Vishnu and Shiva to test Anasuya's devotion to her husband. Trimurti transformed themselves into three old mendicants. They went to the hermitage where Anasuya was living and sought alms from her. When Anasuya was about to serve them food they told her that they had taken a vow whereby they could not accept alms from a person wearing clothes. As it was a sin to refuse alms to mendicants she prayed to her and sprinkled a little 'paatha theertham' on the three old beggars. They were all immediately transformed into babies. She then threw off her clothes and offered them food.

The Goddesses learnt about what had happened. They pleaded with Anasuya to grant them 'maankalya biksha' (gift of married life) and to give them back their husbands. Anasuya showed them the three babies. The Devis ran to the cradle and picked one baby each. Anasuya then prayed to her to restore them back to their original form. Surprisingly Sri Vishnu was in Lakshmi's embrace, Shiva in Parvati's lap and Saraswati with Brahmadev. They accepted that Anasuya's fame as the chestiest woman on earth was justified. Thus the Trimurti came to be represented by the Lingam at Suchindram; the bottom represents Brahmadev, the middle represents Vishnu and the top Shiva.

There is another lore associated with this temple. Once in ancient time God Indra was infatuated with Ahilya, the wife of Rishi Gautama. One night he came to the hermitage where Gautama was living. He played a trick. He crowed like a cock indicating the approach of dawn. Rishi Gautama thinking that dawn was imminent awoke from his sleep. He then went to the river for his ablutions prior to commencing his prayers. Realising that it was too dark for dawn and too early for morning to break he returned to his hut. In the meantime Indra took the physical appearance of Rishi Gautama, approached Ahilya and satisfied his desire. Rishi Gautama returned to his home. He was enraged when he saw his wife in another man's embrace. He cursed the man that his entire body be covered with 'yoni'. He also cursed his wife Ahilya to become a statue of stone.

In order to get rid of his curse Indra went to Gnanaranya and prayed to the Trimurti. Soon he was rid of his curse and transformed into his original form. He then built a temple and installed the Lingam to represent the Trimurti. The Lingam came to be known as "Sthanumalayan" (Sthanu means Shiva, Mal means Vishnu and ayan means Brahmadev). This uniqueness of the Lingam (three gods in one deity image) has made this temple famous in India. This unique Lingam is the principle deity of this temple. The place came to be known as Suchindram (the place where Indra was purified) and the temple as Suchindram temple.

After a long walk we were already standing inside the temple. In order to see the main deity I had to take out my shirt and banyan. Soon we stood before the unique Lingam comprising Brahmadev at the bottom, Vishnu at the middle and Shiva at the top. After offering our reverence to the Trinity we spent a few minutes before we were asked to move.

Stepping down from the temple courtyard we look around the temple inside. We could realise it is a huge temple where everything are bigger in shape and size. This hugeness has spelt a calmness and serenity in the ambience. Looking around we found many beautiful sculptures inside mostly of the Dravidian origin.

In the Alankara Mandapam area adjacent to the northern corridor there are four large musical pillars carved out of a single stone. These pillars stand at 18 feet in height. These are an architectural marvelous of the temple grounds. Two of these large pillars have 33 smaller pillars and the other two 25 each. Each of these smaller pillars produces a different musical note when tapped. Unfortunately these pillars are surrounded by iron grills to prevent vandalism. There are an additional 1035 pillars with carvings in the area known as the dancing hall.

Coming out of the 'Alankara Mandapam' we stood face to face with a gigantic figure of Hanuman. The statue stands at 22 feet and is carved of a single granite block. It is one of the tallest statues of its type in India. It depicts 'Vishwaroop". The statue is subjected to purification by butter. There is a fact of historical interest that this statue was buried in the temple in 1740, fearing an attack by the

Tipu Sultan and was subsequently forgotten. It was rediscovered in 1930 and subsequently restored for viewing.

Images of Vigneswari (a feminine form of Vinayaka), Goddess Aram Vallarta Nayaki, Indra Vinayaka, Kala Bhairava and Sakshi Ganapathi are also enshrined.

There is also a Nandi statue, made of mortar and lime, 13 feet tall and 21 feet long. It is one of the biggest Nandi statues in India. There are also various scenes from Ramayana and Mahabharata depicted in various pillars in the temple. There are other carvings and rich sculptures on every pillar and panel throughout the temple, which are of hundred years old. They are still a feast to our eyes and the imaginations.

Suchindram is one of the Ashthadasha Shaktipeeths. This place is where it is believed that the Upper Teeth of Maa Sati fell. The idols are Devi Maa as “Maa Narayani” (wife of Narayan) and Shiva as “Samhara Bhairava” (the destroyer) the protector. At Suchindram, Shiva is locally called Sthanu Shiva.

History to this place dates back in the time when it is said that the Upper teeth of Maa Sati fell on this place. In order to embark the spiritual importance to this place of fall, a temple was constructed. Over the years there are several renovation being carried out on it.

This town along with Kanyakumari was part of Travancore. It became part of Tamil Nadu in 1956. The place is not far from colachel where the historic naval battle between the Dutch and Travancore was fought. Situated between Kanyakumari (11 Km) and Nagarcoil (7 Km) it has an average elevation of only 62 ft from mean sea level.

There are several inscriptions from the period of early and medieval Cholas along with other Pandya rulers in the region. Inscriptions dating back to the 9th century are found in this temple.

The current temple was renovated in the 17th century. It was previously controlled by the Nambudiris, one of the main Namboodiri families called the Thekkumon Madam. Thirumalai Nayak and the Travancore Maharajas, under whose administration the temple remained till Kanyakumari merger with Tamil Nadu, have made many endowments for its upkeep.

Narmada Shondesh

That was the time we were staying at Indore in Madhya Pradesh. Like in the past we decided to take a few days break in this Septembers too. This time we decided to spend our holidays at the hills of Amarkantak, the Holi town of the Hindus.

We travelled from Indore by Narmada Express and got down at a small station named Pendra Road. We visited the station restaurant which was quite clean and modern looking unlike many others. We quickly had our fast lunch with Chhole-Bhature which was very tasty and satisfying. From there we travelled by hired taxi and reached Amarkantak in over an hour. It became dark by then. We checked in our Tent cottage. The location of the hotel was excellent – on the slope of a hill surrounded by forests. In the night we heard howling jackals from the nearby forests. This is our very first experience of staying in a tent house.

Next morning the taxi dropped us before the main entry of a huge temple premise. We had to climb many steps to reach the top temple yard made of stone. On the top we found a large water tank or Kund surrounded by stony platform on all the four sides.

We first visited the Holi Narmada Udgam phenomenon. Inside a smaller temple type building there was a point from where a stream of water seen springing out. This is said to be the Narmada River stream sprang out in the form of a spring and created the vast water tank outside. This tank is believed to be the source of the Narmada River.

There were many big and small temples built around the tank mostly on the north and east side. On the northern flank of the tank was standing a beautiful temple built with white colour stones. The face of the temple was towards the Narmada Udgam Point.

People were standing in a queue to pay their reverence. This is the Mata Narmada temple and locally known as the Shondesh Shakti Peeth (**Fig 17**). It is among the 51 Shakti Peeth of Goddess Adi Shakti (in her incarnation as Devi Sati). It is said that, the Right Buttock of Devi Sati fell here, when Vishnu in order to relieve Lord Shiva from his grief of losing beloved wife Sati, used his 'Sudarshan Chakra' to severe Sati's Body. Here the idol of Adi Shakti is called as 'Narmada' and Lord Shiva is worshipped as 'Bhadrasen'.

We had already kept our shoes, etc. in the taxi. So we readily stood for a while in the small queue. We soon enter the sanctum sanctorum of the Shondesh Shakti Peeth temple.

The temple had beautiful architectures on inside walls, which looked very adorable. In the centre was the idol of Maa Narmada on a silver platform. It was surrounded by the golden 'Mukut', all around. Idols of different Hindu goddesses were there on both sides. We stood for sometimes before the Goddess and offered our reverence to Mata Narmada (Devi Adi Shakti).

After a while we came out of the temple and stood on the Holi Udgam premises. The white stone made temple with ponds all around it produces a picturesque view. Located between the Satpura and Vindhya mountain ranges the beautifully picturesque place is the abode of Gods. It is said whoever dies here gets a place in heaven. Narmada Devi Shondesh Shakthi Peeth is one of the ancient temples and is believed to be 6000 years old. According to the mythology Daksha yajna and Sati self-immolation, it is the holy place where "Right buttock" fell down. It is believed that the Holi Udgam of the Narmada River in this place of Amarkantak added to the charm of the temple and the place as well.

Legend has it: When Shiva destroyed Tripura (three cities) by fire few ashes fell at Kailash, few at Amarkantak and remaining were saved by himself at heaven. It is believed that ashes fell at Amarkantak transformed into crores of Shiv Lingas. But at present we are able to see only one at Jwaleshwar. Because of this holy ashes, it is believed that whoever devotee enters into Mata Narmada Temple their souls will be cleansed.

Narmada Udgam Complex is a walled complex of shrines with the sacred Kund is its main focus, from which the Narmada is believed to have emanated. The white shrines around here sparkle in the sunlight and are situated around two tanks. The water from the holy tanks pours out from a sprout in the form of a gau mukh (literally, cow's mouth).

The temple was built by the Bhonsle kings of Nagpur in the 18th century. It houses a black stone image of the river with large silver eyes. Opposite her chamber is the shrine of the Amarkanteshwar Shivalinga.

Located nearby, a group of 10th-century ruins, known as Karna Math temples stand with towering Shikharas, built by the Kalachuri dynasty of Jabalpur. It is surrounded by shrines that contain icons dedicated to Surya, Vishnu, Gorakhnath and Shivalingas. Every year, on the occasion of Narmada Jayanti, the black-basalt statue of the river goddess is draped in brocade and worshipped by hordes of zealous worshippers.

Chamundeshwari

That was when we were in Mysore on our Special South India trip. It was arranged by the Indian Railway on the occasion of the 125th birth Anniversary of Swami Vivekananda.

After the breakfast we were taken out for sightseeing trip at Mysore by bus arranged by the Railway team. Our first stop was at Chamundeshwari temple.

The Chamundeshwari Temple is considered as a Shaktipeeth and is one of the 18 Maha Shaktipeeths. It is known as Krouncha Pitham as the region was known as Krouncha Puri in Puranic times. It is said that the hair of Sati Devi fell here. This has created the Abode of Sati Devi or Goddess Adi Parashakti at this sacred place.

The temple is situated on the top of the Chamundi Hills at an elevation of 3000 feet from MSL. Chamundi Hills is about 13 km from the city centre of Mysore. The Shrine is said to be over 1000 years old. The Original shrine is said to have been built in the 12th century or early by the Hoysala rulers. Shrine was small initially. Its fame spread far and wide when the Wodeyar clan took over the reign of Mysuru in 1399 AD. Wodeyars were worshipper of Goddess Adi Shakti. In her incarnation as Durga she is the slayer of demons Chanda and Munda, as well as the invincible king of demons Mahishasura. She became known as Devi Chamundeshwari. Wodeyars accepted Goddess Chamundeshwari as their guardian deity. Since then Devi Chamundeshwari has become the presiding deity of the state and is commonly known as Naada Devathe.

Its tower was probably built by the Vijayanagar rulers of the 17th century. Initially it was only the hilly track to access the temple. In 1659 AD a steep staircase of one thousand steps was built to reach the Shrine which is said to be at elevation of 838 ft. Our bus took us close to the temple complex through the motorable road built separately. After coming out of the bus we climbed up to the temple site through the hill slope. The old staircase steps are also seen being used by many. Very close to the main temple we found a huge idol of Nandi made of black granite in front of a small Shiva temple in the adjacent place. This Nandi is over 15 feet high, and 24 feet long and around its neck are exquisite bells.

We walked up to the plain courtyard outside the temple. A huge enchanting seven-tier Gopura (Pyramidal tower) did welcome us. We were overwhelmed with the art and the mammoth size of the gate. In the complex courtyard we took entry ticket from the counter. Then we stood in the queue. After sometime we could enter the temple premises. As for the architecture of the Chamundi temple, it is a quadrangular edifice constructed as per Dravidian style (**Fig 18**). It has a main door, an entrance, Navranga Hall, Antharala Mandapa, Sanctum Sanctorum, and Prakaram. We saw a Vimana (small tower) on the top of the sanctum sanctorum. We found there are seven (the tower at the entrance) golden kalash (sacred urns) placed on to the Shikhara. On stepping inside the temple, we saw a small statue of Ganesha. After walking a few steps, a flagstaff of the Goddess, her footprints and a small image of Lord Ganesha on the silver-plated doorway statue of Nandi can be seen in front of the sanctum sanctorum. Also, an image of Hanuman can be seen close to the holy chamber. The twin Dikpalakas – Nandini and Kamalini are also present at the entrance. Before the sanctum sanctorum, a statue of Bhairav, a manifestation of Lord Shiva, is also visible.

The sanctum sanctorum houses a stone image of Durga in her seated pose and having eight-hands. Legend has it that the image was enthroned by the immortal sage Markandeya. An image of Sri Chakra, which symbolises the Great Goddess herself, is also worshipped in the temple. A number of priests were found engaged in worshipping the goddess. Coconuts, fruits and flowers are offered to the goddess by the pilgrims. Delicious laddoos are also seen being offered.

We offered our reverence to the Goddess and stood before her for a little while seeking her blessing before we were being pushed to move ahead.

The legend about the Chamundi hills and the temple goes like this: Skanda Purana, the holy ancient texts, talks of a pious place known as Trimuta Kshetra. This place is believed to be enclosed by eight hills. Chamundi Hills is believed to be one of those eight sacred hills. Long ago, the hill was also known as Mahabaladri to adulate Shiva. Shiva is worshipped in the Mahabaleswara Temple, the oldest shrine situated atop the eight holy hills in the region. Later, however, the hill was renamed as Chamundi Hills to honour, Goddess Chamundi, one of the main protagonists of the Devi Mahamaya. Goddess Chamundi is a manifestation of Devi Parvati, the divine spouse of Shiva. The temple of Goddess Chamundi possesses supreme powers to grant boons.

After spending sometimes we came out of sanctum sanctorum and stood on the temple courtyard. We found a 6-feet-long statue of Maharaja Krishnaraja Wodeyar III along with his three queens namely Ramavilasa, Lakshmivilasa and Krishnavilasa present in the shrine.

Krishnaraja Wodeyar III renovated the temple in 1827 A.D. The blessed king also installed a Singha-Vahana (mount of lion), cars for the deities and loads of other valuables to the temple. The cars donated by the king are still used during special religious occasions and grand events.

While coming down on our way we found a huge statue of the demon Mahishasura, holding a sword and a serpent in his hands. The Chamundi Village is also situated quite close to the shrine. A host of amenities for the welfare of pilgrims are present in and around the temple. Free drinking water and facilities for offering special worship and commuting from City Bus Stand to Chamundi Hill are also available.

Our stoppage at the Chamundeshwari temple was for about 2 hours. It was a pleasing experience witnessing such overwhelming faith on Goddess Adi Shakti.

Chandrabhaga

That year we spent our autumn holidays in south-west Gujarat trip covering places like Veraval, Chorwad, Somnath and Junagadh. That was one of our excellent memorable vacation trips.

We travelled from Baroda to Veraval via Ahmedabad. We reached Veraval early morning. After getting refreshed we had breakfast. Then with the help of hotel staff we hired an Auto for sight-seeing Somnath and its surroundings. The distance of 9 km was covered in half an hour. At first we had our reverence paid to Shiva at his world famous historical Jyotirling Shrine. The auto driver after parking his auto guided us voluntarily. We completed our visit to the shrine in about an hour or so. We took many photographs of the shrine and the surroundings from outside only. Then we visited the Arabian Ocean at the back of the temple.

After completing our stay at the temple we started for other sight – seeing spots. Our first stop was at Triveni Sangam Ghat about 1 km from the Somnath temple site. The Ghat oversees the confluence of three rivers – Hiran, Kapil and the mythical Saraswati. This is a very sacred place for the Hindus. The confluence of rivers then empties together into the Arabian Sea. These stages of rivers where they meet and then flow together to the sea symbolize human birth, life and death. It is said that if one takes a bath in this confluence then one's all sins will be washed away and one will be pardoned from rebirth. Mentions of the Triveni Ghat are available in the Holi scriptures of the Ramayana, the Mahabharata and the Hindu Puranas.

According to the Puranas Krishna after getting struck at his foot by an arrow of a hunter visited this place. It is believed that Lord Krishna had left his material body here at this place and his Samadhi is also located here.

We walked down some distance towards the western end of the Ghat behind the temple of Parashurama on the Triveni check-dam road. We reached in front of the boundary wall of a temple. Inside was located the Goddess Chandrabhaga Shaktipeeth (locally known as Kali Mandir).Reaching inside the Kali Mandir we found no worshippers. Only a priest was seating inside the Garbhagriha. This was the Chandrabhaga Shaktipeeth, one of 51 Shaktipeeths (**Fig 19**). It is believed by the Hindus that abdominal or the stomach of Devi Sati had fallen at this place and thus it became the sacred abode of Goddess Adi Parashakti or Adi Shakti. The temple is near to the Samshan land (Burning Ghat). A temple of Shiva was also seen in adjacent place. The Deity of the temple is known as Vakratund Bhairav, stood as the protector of Devi Sati.

The temple is popularly known as Prabhas Shakti Peeth, Maa Maha Laxmi Mandir. We offered our reverence to Goddess Chandrabhaga and stayed for some time. Then we came out of the temple and look around for a while.

There was a temple or Chhatri dedicated to Krishna. Hindus believe that he was cremated at this place. Then there were Gita Mandir and Lakshmi Narayan temple on the banks of the Triveni Ghat.

We felt sad to know that local people were not aware of it being a Shaktipeeth. This may be the only one in the country. We did not stay further at the Ghat and moved ahead for our next sight-seeing spot.

Maya Devi

That was sometime in the mid-Sept 2005. We stopped over in Haridwar on our way to visit Gangotri Dham in that trip. During our stay at Haridwar on the first day we visited many pilgrimage centres there.

We availed the ropeway trip to complete our visit to Goddess Mansa Devi Temple atop the Bilwa Parvat (altitude 600 ft) on the Shivalik hills. After offering our reverence at this Siddhi Peeth we came back to the city in an hour. We knew about the existence of a Shaktipeeth in Haridwar. But we did not know the exact location of the same. In the morning before starting our local sightseeing we however got some idea about the location from the hotel manager. We hired an auto and asked him to take us to Maya Devi Temple, our revered Shaktipeeth. Maya Devi Temple is a Hindu temple dedicated to goddess Maya in the holy city of Haridwar. It is believed that the heart and navel of goddess Sati fell in the region where the temple stands today. Although the name does not appear in the list of 51 Shaktipeeths but Hindus consider this temple as a Shakti Peetha.

Our auto was passing through the Upper road at Birla Ghat near to the Har-ki-pauri. We came to the eastern side of the Har-ki-Pauri. The locality appeared to be a very normal residential place and no pilgrim like activity were noticed anywhere. However as we entered an interior lane we saw many shops selling flowers and puja materials indicating the presence of the temple nearby. Soon our auto stopped before the temple looking gate of a house. We got down there and released the auto. The beautiful gate was having some attraction which made me to take a photograph.

Then we entered the temple premises. It had a long walking corridor on both sides of which a few flower shops were available. We bought a flower-set as is offered to the Goddess. The seller asked us to keep our footwears there. Fortunately number of devotees were moderate. With bare feet we walked inside the main temple hall and reached up to the Garbh-griha.

We saw in the inner shrine the deities Maya Devi in the centre, Goddess Kali on the left, Maa Kamakhya on the right (**Fig 20**). Idols of two other Goddesses were also there but could not be seen. They are also believed to be the other forms of Goddess Adi Shakti. Goddess Maya is the Adhisthatri deity of Haridwar. She is a three-headed and four-armed deity. We handed over our flower set to the Priest and offered our prayers to the goddess Adi Shakti. The tranquility of the ambient made us feel lost for a while. Priest then returned to us some Pushp and Prasad which we collected. We walked around there for sometime in the peaceful environment of the temple and then came out.

Haridwar was previously known as Mayapuri in reverence to this deity. The temple is a Siddha Peetha. In this Divine Center worshipping fulfils one's desire. It is one of three such Siddha Peethas located in Haridwar, the other two being Chandi Devi Temple and Mansa Devi Temple. The temple dates back to the eleventh century AD. It is one of the three ancient temples of Haridwar of that period which are still intact, the other two being Narayana-shila and Bhairava Temple. We offered our prayers to the Goddess and completed Darshan to the temple in half an hour. From there we walked down and reached the Har-ki – Pauri. We crossed the Ganges and came to otherside to find a restaurant to complete our launch.

Famous Chinese traveler Huan Tsang mentioned about the city of Haridwar in his travel diary that dates back to about 629 AD. That was the period of reign of King Harshavardhan (590 – 647 AD). The evidences mentioned in the diary still exist in Mayapur located a little south of the present city. During the said period many smaller kingdoms were emerging in the northern and central India. Although the exact name of the builder of the temple is not known, but it was believed to have been rebuilt in the 11 th Century. Then late in the 13th century (in the year 1399) a Turkish Invader found out the Holi city of Haridwar and invaded it for the purpose of looting its treasures. Later, in the 16th century 'Ain – e – Akbari' a book written during Akbar's reign did mention the city as Maypuri. The foremost noted evidence of the present day name Haridwar comes from a Nobel named Thomas Coryant, during the rule of the Mughal Emperor Jahangir (son of Akbar) in the 17th century.

We visited Goddess Maya Devi temple at Haridwar comfortably in a cool and peaceful manner. The environment did induce my mind in a manner which was very similar to what I used to feel in my childhood. Many Hindus consider this Holi place as a Shaktipeeth even though it does not appear in the list of 51 Shaktipeeths. It was a pleasant trip still remembering vividly.

Trisrota Bhramari

After completing our trip to Kalimpong we were on our way to Darjeeling. In the bus that we were travelling by, we came to know from a co-passenger about the presence of a Shaktipeeth in Jalpaiguri district. The location of it is in Bodaganj just at distance of 30 km from NJP station.

On the day of our return trip to Kolkata we started from Darjeeling early in the morning to have adequate time in hand to take a chance to see the Shrine. We reached New Jalpaiguri station by 9 o' clock. After keeping our luggage in the cloak room we finished our breakfast. We came out of the station and hire a taxi for up-down trip to the Bodaganj Shaktipeeth and back. We could start our trip at 10 AM. Our taxi first cross Gora more and take the Gajol Doba road. In half an hour we reach Gatebazar point and take right turn to travel via Belakoba road. In next half an hour we reached Bodaganj. After travelling by the side of the river Tista for some time the taxi left us at little distance away from the temple. The road ahead is the village road.

Nestled in the midst of the lush green Baikunthapur forest, Bodaganj is a small village about 40 km from Siliguri town. We walk down the village road and reached the temple complex through a big welcome gate. We walk down the bricks clad road covering a vast forest area and finally reached the main temple.

A stone image of Ganesh welcomes us at the main temple gate. The hall has an idol of Goddess Durga with eight hands and beautifully ornamented. In front of her there are a few pitchers containing flowers. Beside those there was a stool on which kept two feet of goddess made of brass which is regularly worshipped. On her right there was an idol of Shiva. Walking down a few steps below the room we reached the Garvgriha (Sanctum sanctorum) of Goddess Bhramari Mata. We found goddess is seated on a lion (**Fig 21**). Her body is in dark colour. In front of her idol there was the stony left foot of her which is seen regularly worshipped. We paid our reverence to Goddess Bhramari Mata (local name of Goddess Sati the form of Adi Shakti) and spent some time there to dip ourselves in the peace and tranquillity of the serene place.

Then we come out of the Garvgriha and took a round of the temple premises. We walked down the steps to reach the bank of the river Tista on which the temple is situated. Long ago (till 18th century AD) the river used to be called as Trisrota River as it used to flow in three streams viz. the Karatoa in the east, the Purnavaba in the west and the Atrai in the central part. Over this long period combined streams named as the Trisrota become known as the river Tista. From the old name of Trisrota the Shaktipeeth came to be known as Trisrota Shaktipeeth.

This temple is one of the 51 Shaktipeeths. It is said that left leg of Sati (the human incarnation of Goddess Adi Shakti) had fallen at this place near the Tista River, when Vishnu in order to relieve Shiva from the grief of losing his beloved wife Sati, used his 'Sudarshan Chakra' to incise Sati's corpse. Here the idol of Goddess Adi Shakti is worshipped as Mata Bhramari.

The exact date of the temple's creation is still unknown as this is a Shakti Peeth that had been formed centuries back. History to this place dates back in the time when this temple was constructed. The temple is a one storied, red coloured structure enshrining the idol of Devi Bhramari and Ishwara. This shrine is considered to be central heart chakra of Devi Bhramari, possessing in 12 petals. This works as the guard or antibodies to the humans to heal from any kind of disease. The chakra is the reason for the Kundalini Sadhana observed here. As per the ancient scriptures, Bhramari Devi – the manifestation of Devi Durga exists in the Chakra to protect the people from any kind of external attack by the viruses or bacteria. Bhramari is the Hindu goddess of bees. She is an incarnation of the goddess Adi Shakti in Shaktism and is primarily regarded to be a form of Lakshmi.

Bhramari means 'the goddess of bees', or 'the goddess of black bees'. The goddess is associated with bees, hornets, and wasps, which cling to her body, and is thus typically depicted as emanating bees and hornets from her four hands. The legend associated with the manifestation of Goddess Adi Shakti as Mata Bhramari is as follows:

In the land of Nethersthal of the Daityas, there lived a powerful Asura named Arunasura. He despised the Devas, and sought above all else to conquer these deities. He went to the banks of the Ganges in the Himalayas, and practiced a very strict penance to Brahma, believing him to be the protector of the Daityas.

Observing his penance and resolve and on his request, Brahma saw it just to bless Arunasura with the boon of not meeting his end at any war, nor by any arms or weapons, nor by any man or any woman, by any biped or quadruped creature, or any combination of the two. Confident by the blessings Arunasura called on all the other Daityas living in the nether regions for the final battle against the deities above. On receipt of the message of the ensuing attack Devas were nervous. Indra trembled with fear and along with other Devas met Brahma and Vishnu for finding a way out.

While the deities conferred, Arunasura and his army invaded Devaloka. Daitya Arunasura used the power of his penances to assume various forms and seized possession of the Chandra, Surya, Yama, Agni, and all the elemental deities. All these deities, dislodged from their stations, visited Kailash to seek help from Shiva. He advised them to seek blessings of Goddess Adi Parashakti. The goddess was aware of Aruna's blessing and devised a plan to kill the Daitya with the help of six-legged creatures.

After taking control of all the celestial regions, Arunasura's next intention was to attack Kailash directly. Shiva and his sons confronted him at the foot of the mountain. They tried to defeat him, but were unsuccessful. Even Shiva was unable to defeat him. Adi Shakti then appeared behind Shiva, and grew to a massive size, emanating bees from her four hands. Her three eyes shone like the sun, the moon, and the eternal fire Agni. She closed her eyes in concentration, summoning forth countless bees, hornets, wasps, flies, termites, mosquitoes and spiders from the skies. They crawled onto her body and clung onto her, merging with her to create the divine form of Bhramari.

In the battle that ensued, the Daityas' swords were blocked by Bhramari's massive size, while her other arms inflicted damage on the massive army. The bees, hornets, wasps, flies, termites, mosquitoes and spiders, which clung to her then emanated forth in a wave over the ranks. When Arunasura was the last Daitya remaining on battlefield, she retreated and sent out all of the insects to attack him. They crawled all over him and ripped open each part of his body: his chests, back and belly, arms, hands, fingers, legs, feet, and toes were all torn apart. Soon after seeing Arunasura's great fall, the insects returned to Bhramari and clung on her again. The deities, who were in awe of this new form, praised Goddess Adi Shakti. On the successful decimation of the Daityas, all Devas were able to return to their celestial abodes.

Hindu Purana the Devi Bhagavata Purana records the exploits of the goddess Bhramari in detail. The salutations offered to her in the Markandeya Purana indicate that she is a form of the goddess of prosperity, Lakshmi. She is also briefly alluded to in the Devi Mahatmya. In the Lakshmi Tantra, Lakshmi declares – "During the sixtieth era there will be one demon, called Aruṇa who will do much harm to men and sages. Then I shall appear in bee-form incorporating innumerable bees, and I shall slay the mighty demon and rescue the three worlds. From then on people will praise me forever and address me as Bhramari."

As known in Hinduism, Goddess Bhramari's central heart 'chakra', possessing 12 petals, builds the antibodies to guard humans from disease and from external attacks of negativities like bacteria or virus.

We completed our visit to this Shaktipeeth in two hours. It was difficult to leave this beautiful serene place as Devi Bhramari Mata had spreaded on us a cool wraps of love and affection.

Photographs

Devi Kamakhya Shaktipeeth

Fig.1 Temple Premises

Fig.2 Image of Goddess Dakshina kali

Fig. 3 Goddess Vimala

Fig. 4 Tara Tarini Temple

Goddess Taratarini in the Temple

Idol of Goddess Tara Tarini

Fig.5 Yajna Place

Fig. 6 Goddess Vishalakshi

Devi Jwalaji Shaktipeeth

Fig. 7 Eternal Flame

Chintpurni Shaktipeeth

Fig. 8 Stone cut idol of Mata Chhinnamasta

Fig. 9 Devi Chintpurni Shaktipeeth – Garbhagriha

Fig. 10 Maa Vindhyavasini

Devi Gadkalika Shaktipeeth

Fig. 11 Garbhagriha

Fig. 12 Bhramaramba Devi Shaktipeeth

Maa Kiriteshwari Shaktipeeth

Fig. 13 Garbhagriha

Fig. 14 Devi Jayadurga Shaktipeeth Tied with Vaidyanath Jyotirling

Fig. 15 Devi Amman Shaktipeeth

Fig. 16 Devi Suchindran Shaktipeeth

Maa Narmade Shaktipeeth

Fig. 17 Garbhagriha

Fig.18 Chamundeshwari TempleChamundeshwari Devi temple

Triveni Sangam Ghat

Fig. 19 Chandrabhaga Shaktipeeth

Maya Devi temple

Fig.20 Garbhagriha

Goddess Bhramari Devi

Fig. 21 Trisrota Bhramari Devi Temple

Annexure I: Map of India showing the Shaktipeeths

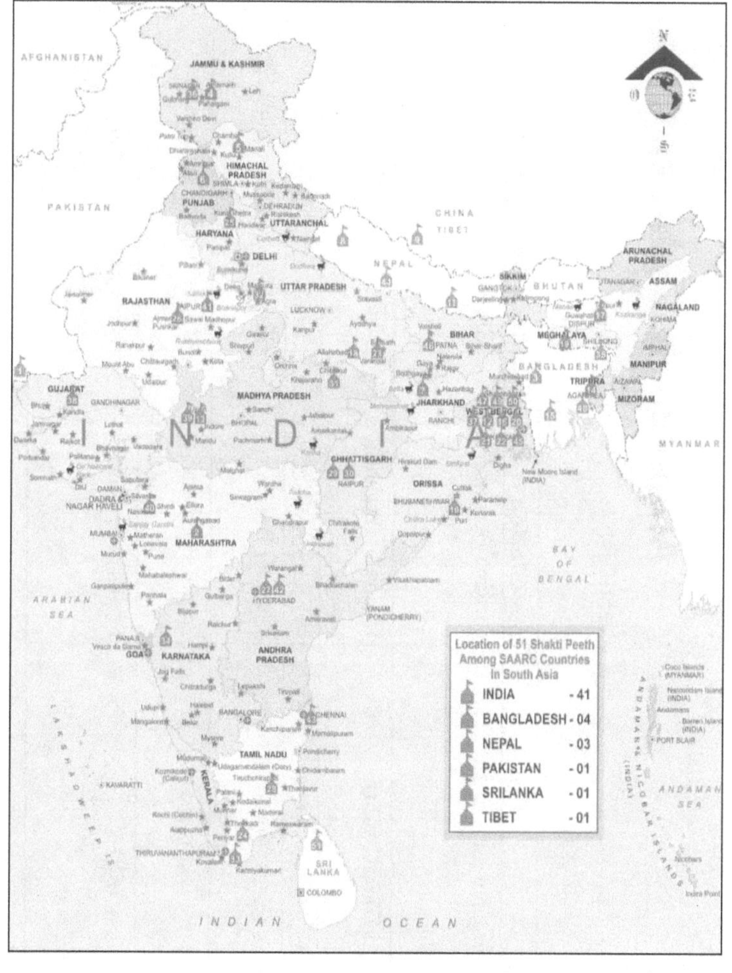

Fig. 22 Map of Shaktipeeth

Annexure II: Eighteen Great Shaktipeeths

	Place	Appellation	Body Part	Shakti	Temple
1	Trincomalee (Sri Lanka)	Sankari Peetham	Groin	Sankari devi	part of Koneswaram temple (Destroyed)
2	Kanchi (Tamil Nadu)	Kanchi Kamakodi Peetham	Naval	Kamakshi	Kamakshi Amman Temple
3	Pandua, Hoogly district (WB)	Pradyumna Peetham	Stomach	Shrinkala	
4	Mysore (Karnataka)	Krounja Peetham	Hair	Chamundeshwari	Chamundeshwari Temple
5	Alampur (Telangana)	Yogini Peetham	Upper teeth	Jogulamba (Yogaamba)	
6	Srisailam, (AP)	Srisaila Peetham	Neck part	Bhramaramba	Bhramaramba Mallikarjuna Temple

7	Kolhapur (Maharashtra)	Shri Peetham	Left eye	Mahalakshmi	Mahalakshmi Temple, Kolhapur
8	Hirvai (Yatmal, Maharashtra)		Back part	Ekavirika	Ekavira Temple
9	Ujjain (MP)	Ujjaini Peetham	Elbow	Mahakali	
10	Pithapuram (AP)	Pushkarini Peetham	Left hand	Puruhutika	
11	Jajpur (Odisha)	Oddyana Peetham	Naval	Biraja	Biraja Temple
12	Draksharamam (AP)	Draksharama Peetham	Navel	Manikyamba devi	
13	Guwahati (Assam)	Kamarupa Peetham	Vulva	Kamarupa	Kamakhya Temple
14	Prayaga (Uttar Pradesh)	Prayaga Peetham	Fingers	Madhaveswari devi	
15	Jwalamukhi (Himachal Pradesh)	Jwalamukhi Peetham	Head Part	Jwalamukhi	Jwalamukhi Temple
16	Gaya (Bihar)	Gaya Peetham	Breast part	Sarva-mangala	Mangla Gauri Temple
17	Varanasi (Uttar Pradesh)	Varanasi Peetham	Throat	Vishalakshi	Vishalakshi Temple
18	Jammu and Kashmir	Sharada Peetham	Lips	Sharada	Sharada Peeth *(Destroyed)

[*] Sharada Peeth temple is currently non-existent. Only ruins are found in these places. Its ruins are near the Line of Control (LOC).

Among these, the Shakthi Peethas at Kamakhya, Gaya and Ujjain are regarded as the most sacred as they symbolise the three most important aspects of the Mother Goddess viz. Creation (Kamarupa Devi), Nourishment (Sarvamangala Devi/Mangalagauri) and Annihilation (Mahakali Devi).

When observed carefully one can see that they lie in a perfect straight line from Kamakhya to Ujjain via Gaya, symbolizing that every creation in this universe will annihilate one day without fail.

Another source provides following list of the Ashthadasha Maha-Shaktipeeths, which appears to be differing from the above table.

Sri Sankari Peeths (at Lanka)

Sri Simhika Peeths (at Simhala)

Sri Manika Peeths (at Dakshavati)

Sri Sudkala Peeths (At Petapur)

Sri Bhramaramba Peeths (Srisailam)

Sri Vijaya Peeths (Vijayapura)

Sri Mahalakshmi Peeths (Kolhapur)

Sri Kamakshi Peeths (Kancheepuram)

Sri Kuchananda Peeths (Salagrama)

Sri Viraja Peeths (Odyana, Jajpur)

Sri Bhadreswari Peeths (Harmyagiri)

Sri Mahakali Peeths (Ujjayini)

Sri Vindhyavasini Peeths (Vindhyachal)

Sri Mahayogi Peeths (Ahicchatra)

Sri Kanyaka Peeths (Kanya Kubja)

Sri Visalakshi Peeths (Kashi)

Sri Saraswati Peeths (Kashmira)

Sri Abhirama Peeths (Padmagiri, Dindigul)

(Ref: Ashthadasha Sanskrit Stotram is available in the said Purana).

Annexure III: The Shaktipeeths at a Glance

Sr. No.	Place	Body Part or Ornament	Shakti
1	Amarnath, Chandanwari 16 km by walk from Pahalgam, 94 km by Bus from Srinagar.	Throat	Mahamaya
2	At a village also named as Attahas or Ashtahas around 2 km east of Labhpur village road in the district of Birbhum	Lips	Phullara
3	Bahula, on the banks of Ajay river at Ketugram, 8 km from Katwa, Burdwan	Left arm	Goddess Bahula
4	Bakreshwar, on the banks of Paaphara river, 24 km from Siuri Town, Birbhum, 7 km from Dubrajpur Rly station	Portion between the eyebrows	Mahishmardini
5	Bhairavparvat, at Bhairav hills on the banks of Shipra river in the city of Ujjaini. Local People call this temple as Gadkalika.	Elbow	Avanti

6	Bhabanipur, located in the Upazilla of Sherpur, Bogra, Rajshahi Division. Also located at Karatoyatat, it is about 28 km distance from the town of Sherpur.	Left anklet (ornament)	Aparna
7	Chhinnamastika Shaktipeeth at Chintpurni, in Una District of Himachal Pradesh	Feet	Chhinnamastika
8	Gandaki, Pokhara, Nepal about 125 km on the banks of Gandaki river where Muktinath temple is situated	Temple	Gandaki Chandi
9	Goddess Bhadrakali on banks of the Godavari in Nasik city	Chin (2 parts)	Bhramari
10	Hinglaj, southern Baluchistan a few hours North-east of Gawadar and about 125 km towards North-west from Karachi	Bramharandhra (Part of the head)	Kottari
11	Jayanti at Nartiang village in the Jaintia Hills district. This Shakti Peetha is locally known as the Nartiang Durga Temple.	Left thigh	Jayanti
12	Jessoreswari, at Ishwaripur, Shyamnagar Upazila, Khulna, Bangladesh. Temple was built by Maharaja Pratapaditya, whose capital was Ishwaripur.	Palms of hands and soles of the feet	Jashoreshwari

13	Jwalaji, Kangra from Pathankot alight at Jwalamukhi Road Station from there 20 km	Tongue	Siddhida (Ambika)
14	Kalipeeth, (Kalighat, Kolkata)	Right Toes	Kalika
15	Kalmadhav on the banks of Sone river in a cave over hills near to Amarkantak	Left buttock	Kali
16	Kamgiri, Kamakhya, in the Neelachal hills near Guwahati	Genitals	Kamakhya
17	Kankalitala, on the banks of Kopai River 10 km north-east of Bolpur station in Birbhum district, Devi locally known as Kankaleshwari	Pelvis	Devgarbha
18	Kanyashram of Balaambika – Kumari Bhagavathy Devi temple in Kanyakumari, the southernmost tip of mainland India Tamil Nadu	Back	Sarvani
19	Karnat, Brajeshwari Devi, Kangra	Both ears	Jayadurga
20	Kireet at Kireetkona village, 3 km from Lalbagh Court Road, Murshidabad	Crown	Vimla
21	Locally known as Anandamayee Temple. Ratnavali, on the banks of Ratnakar river at Khanakul, district Hooghly	Right Shoulder	Kumari

22	Locally known as Bhramari Devi. In Jalpaiguri near a small village Boda on the bank of river Teesta or Tri-shrota (combination of three flows) mentioned in Puranas	Left leg	Bhramari
23	Manas, under Tibet at the foot of Mount Kailash in Lake Mansarovar, a piece of Stone	Right hand	Dakshayani
24	Manibandh, at Gayatri hills near Pushkar 11 km north-west of Ajmer. People know this temple as Chamunda Mata Temple.	Wrists	Gayatri
25	Mithila, near Janakpur railway station on the border of India and Nepal	Left shoulder	Uma
26	Nainativu (Manipallavam), Northern Province, Sri Lanka. Located 36 km from the ancient capital of the Jaffna kingdom, Nallur. The idol was consecrated and worshipped by Indra. The protagonist, Rama and antagonist, Ravana have offered obeisances to the Goddess. Naga and Garuda of the epic Mahabharata resolved their longstanding feuds after worshipping this Goddess.	Silambu (Anklets)	Indrakshi / Bhuvaneswari)
27	Guhyeshwari Temple, near Pashupatinath Nepal	Both Knees	Mahashira

28	On Chandranath hill, Sitakunda station of Chittagong Division, Bangladesh. The famous Chandranath Temple on the top of the hill is the Bhairav temple of this Shakti Peetha, not the Shakti Peeth itself.	Right arm	Bhawani
29	Panchsagar near Lohaghat, Champawat (Uttarakhand), 100 km from Tanakpur.	Lower teeth	Varahi
30	Prabhas, 4 km from Veraval station near Somnath temple, Junagadh. Locally known as Kali Mandir, near Triveni Sangam.	Stomach	Chandrabhaga
31	Prayaga Madhaveswari known as Alopi Mata near Sangam at Allahabad	Finger	Lalita
32	Present day Kurukshetra town or Thanesar ancient Sthaneshwar	Ankle bone	Savitri/ BhadraKali
33	Ramgiri, at Chitrakoot on the Jhansi Manikpur railway line in UP	Right breast	Shivani
34	Sainthia, locally known as Nandikeshwari temple. Only 1.5 km from the railway station under a banyan tree within a boundary wall, Birbhum district	Necklace	Nandini
35	Sarvashail or Godavaritir, at Kotilingeswar temple on the banks of Godavari river near Rajahmundry, AP	Cheeks	Rakini or Vishweshwari

36	Naina Devi temple in Bilaspur district of Himachal Pradesh	Eyes	Mahishmardini
37	Shondesh, at the source point of Narmada River in Amarkantak	Right buttock	Narmada
38	Shri Parvat, near Ladakh, Jammu and Kashmir	Right anklet (ornament)	Shrisundari
39	Shri Shail, at Joinpur village, Dakshin Surma, near Gotatikar, 3 km north-east of Sylhet town, Bangladesh	Neck	Mahalaxmi
40	Shuchi, in a Shiva temple at Suchindrum 11 km on Kanyakumari Trivandrum road	Upper teeth	Narayani
41	Sugandha, situated in Shikarpur, Gournadi, 20 km from Barisal town on the banks of Sonda river, Bangladesh	Nose	Sugandha
42	Udaipur, Tripura, at the top of the hills known as Tripura Sundari temple near Radhakishorepur village, a little distance away from Udaipur town	Right leg	Tripura Sundari
43	Ujaani, at Mangalkot 16 km from Guskara station under Burdwan district	Right wrist	Mangal Chandika
44	Varanasi at Manikarnika Ghat on banks of the Ganges at Kashi	Earring	Vishalakshi & Manikarni
45	Vibhash, at Tamluk under district East Medinipur, WB	Left ankle	Kapalini (Bhimarupa)

46	Virat, near Bharatpur, Rajasthan	Left toes	Ambika
47	Vrindavan, near new bus stand on Bhuteshwar road within Bhuteshwar Mahadev Temple, Katyayanipeeth. Vrindavan.	Ringlets of hair	Uma
48	Jalandhar, from Jalandhar Cantonment Station to Devi Talab.	Left Breast	Tripurmalini
49	Baidyanath Dham, Deoghar, Jharkhand	Heart	Jaya Durga
50	Biraja Temple in Jajpur, Odisha	Bamonbonsham (Navel)	Biraja
51	Jugaadya, at Kshirgram near Kaichar under Burdwan district	Great Toe	Jugaadya

Key Explanatory Note

Srishti: The Sanskrit word for creation is *Srishti*. This means projecting a gross thing from a subtle substance. This does not mean bringing out existence from non-existence or creating something from nothing. Hindus declare that non-existence can never be the source of creation. Thus, the universe is more accurately said to be the projection of the Supreme Being rather than a creation. This matches with the Hindu belief that the universe has no beginning or end, but follows a cosmic cycle of creation and dissolution which was the idea as old as Hinduism echoing the "oscillating universe" model. Recently developed 'the Cyclical Model' by a few foreign institutes confirmed that there could be a timeless cycle of expansion and contraction. Another view of creation expressed in Hindu literature the Bhagavad Gita that the universe was not created, it will not be destroyed. It simply is.

Maya: Enlightening us on worldly illusion Hindu priest Ramakrishna called the world as "The Great Stage of Play of the Divine Mother of the universe." We are all creatures of spirit with various coatings of matter hiding the spirit from the light. As we do our Karmic roles in this great play, we remove the coatings of matter and release the light within us. The more light we accumulate within us, the more we can see the light hidden in other people and things. In reality, the whole world play exists for us to seek God Consciousness. All people are either striving towards the light or hiding from it. Those who are hiding are caught up in the Maya. So, everything which has existence, everything in the phenomenal world is Maya. Maya is thus that cosmic force that presents the infinite Brahman (the Supreme Being) as the finite phenomenal world. Maya is reflected on the individual level by human ignorance of the real nature of the self, which man has mistaken for the empirical ego but which is in reality identical with Brahman.

Primal Energy: Reality behind the veils of Maya lies in seeing everything in the universe as a differentiation or gradation of Primal Energy. Primal Energy is the Infinite Transcendental Essence which permeates all existence. Thus, at the root of all existence--all Maya lays Primal Energy. Primal Energy is also the Great 'Aum', the word, or even God, if you will. Thus, when Hindus clasp their hands together and bow towards each other, they are saying, in effect, "The God within me greets the God within you."

Shaktism: In Shakta theology (an essential section of Hinduism), the feminine and masculine are interdependent realities, represented with Ardhnaarishwar icon. Shaktas conceive the Goddess as the supreme, ultimate, eternal reality of all existence, or same as the Brahman concept of Hinduism. She is considered to be simultaneously the source of all creation, its embodiment and the energy that animates and governs it, and that into which everything will ultimately dissolve. In Shaktism theology Brahman is static Shakti and Shakti is dynamic Brahman. Shaktism views the Devi as the source, essence and substance of everything in creation. Shaktism focus on the Divine Feminine does not imply a rejection of masculine. It rejects male-female, soul-body, transcendent-immanent dualism, considering nature as divine. Devi is considered to be the cosmos itself – she is the embodiment of energy, matter and soul, the motivating force behind all action and existence in the material universe.

Brahmaloka: It is the abode of goddess Saraswati and Brahmadev, the creator goddess and god. Located on Mount Meru, it is also referred to as ***Satyaloka*** (satya meaning truth, loka meaning world, hence meaning true world). In the Puranas Brahmaloka is described as a flower-filled garden signifying only the absolute reality of infinite Pure Consciousness-Bliss, the highest of the joyful worlds a person might attain. In Satyaloka, there are lotus flowers everywhere. These lotuses are huge, with divine energy flowing out of them. In the center of Brahmaloka, is Brahmapura, a huge palace in which Brahmadev lives in. Below Satyaloka is Tapaloka and above it are the end of the material universe and the start of the Vaikunth planets.

Brahmadev: He (in Sanskrit from the verbal root Brih meaning to expand, grow, fructify) is the vivifying expansive force of nature in its eternally periodic Manvantara. He stands for the spiritual evolving or developing energy-consciousness of a solar system which is also called the Egg of Brahmadev (Brahmanda). Brahmadev is called the creator or Logos, but in the theosophical philosophy creator is simply an abstract term or idea, like army. In Burnouf's words "Having evolved himself from the soul of the world, once separated from the first cause, he evaporates with, and emanates all nature out of himself. He does not stand above it, but is mixed up with it; Brahmadev and the universe form one Being, each particle of which is in its essence Brahmadev himself, who proceeded out of himself". According to the Aitareya-Brahmana, Brahmadev as Prajapati (of beings) manifests himself first of all as twelve bodies or attributes, which are represented by the twelve gods, symbolizing 1) fire; 2) the sun; 3) soma, which gives omniscience; 4) all living beings; 5) Vayu, or ether; 6) death, or breath of destruction — Siva; 7) earth; 8) heaven; 9) Agni, the immaterial fire; 10) Aditya, the immaterial and invisible sun; 11) mind; and 12) the great infinite cycle, "which is not to be stopped." Brahmadev in one of his phases therefore is the visible universe, every atom of which is essentially he. Brahmadev "symbolizes personally the collective creators of the World and Men — the universe with all its countless productions of things movable and (seemingly) immovable. He is collectively the Prajapatis, the s of Being; and the four bodies typify the four classes of creative powers which are being Ratri (night) associated with the creation of the asuras; Ahan (day) associated with the gods; Sandhya (evening twilight) associated with the pitris; and Joytsna (dawn or light) associated with the creation of men.

Purusha and Prakriti: The masculine sense when it is the evolving energy of the cosmic egg is Brahmadev. In the beginning Brahmadev was Purusha (spirit) and also Prakriti (matter). It is later that he separated himself into two halves — Brahmadev-Vach (female) and Brahmadev-Viraj (male). Brahmadev in its totality has essentially the aspect of Prakriti, both evolved and unevolved (Mulaprakrti), and also the aspects of spirit and of time. "Brahmadev, as 'the germ of unknown Darkness,' is the material from which all evolves and develops 'as the web from the spider, as foam from the water,' etc. This is only graphic and true, if Brahmadev the 'Creator' is, as a term, derived from the root Brih, to increase or expand. Brahmadev 'expands' and becomes the Universe woven out of his own substance".

Brahma's Yuga concept: One human year is equivalent to one day and night for the Devas. One Deva-Vatsara comprises 360 numbers of Deva days and nights. Thus a Deva-Vatsara consists of 129600 human years. A mythological Chaturyuga is made up of 12,000 Deva-Vatsara i.e. 1555200000 (i.e. 1.5552 billion) human years. A Chaturyuga as the term implies is broken in to 4 Yugas viz., Satyayuga (622.08 million human years), Tretayuga (466.56

million human years), Dwapara Yuga (311.04 million human years) and Kaliyuga (155.52 million human years).

Manu's texts on Yuga: This explains the physical concept and the human relevance of the Yugas. In the first of the Chaturyuga the Satya Yuga, also known as the Golden Age, human beings are said to have direct contact with the divine intelligence emanating from Brahma, the seat of creative power and intelligence in the cosmos. During this age there is no crime and everybody is righteous. All men resemble religious saints. The weather is always pleasant during Satyayuga, there is no mining or agriculture because the Earth produces its own resources, and there is an absence of disease. Everybody is gigantic and big-built, but also virtuous and honest. Everybody lives on for thousands of years.

After the end of the Golden Age, humanity enters a denser era, the Treta Yuga (also known as the Silver Age). In this age, humanity's connection with the source is dimmed. Sacrifices and spiritual practices become necessary to preserve it. During Treta Yuga, humans become slightly less virtuous and righteous. Violent kings are born and cause bloody wars. The weather starts becoming extreme and human starts mining and farming.

In the sequence next era the Dwapara Yuga also known as Bronze Age follows and humanity forgets its divine nature. Empty dogmas arise, along with indulgence in materialism. During this time period, humans, in general, become less strong and able. Diseases become common and humans start fighting each other for power and wealth. The average life span is reduced to a couple of centuries.

In the last of the sequence the humanity enters the Kali Yuga (also known as Iron Age), in which we remain today. Human spirit suffers under gross materialism, ignorance, warfare, stupidity, arrogance, and everything contrary to our divine spiritual potential occurs. "Kali" means "dark", so it is an age of darkness and ignorance. It is the opposite of Satyayuga. Humans become dishonest sinners and commit unbelievable sins. Knowledge is disregarded as useless and the scriptures fade into the past. The wealth and strength of humans are lesser than the previous Yugas. Wealth will be subverted by a few and the rest will struggle to acquire a part. By the end of Kali Yuga, humans will have ruined the environment and their average lifespan dive down to merely 20 years. Thus Manu's texts summarises the Chaturyuga from a pinnacle of light of the Satya Yuga to the ultimate end-point of the process—the darkness of Kalki Yuga.

Manvantara & Universal Cycle (Lifespan of Brahmadev): In Hindu cosmology it is a cyclic period of time identifying the duration, reign, or age of a Manu, the progenitor of mankind. In each Manvantara seven Rishis, certain deities, an Indra, a Manu, and kings (sons of Manu) are created and perish. Each Manvantara is distinguished by the Manu who rules/reigns over it, of which we are currently in the seventh Manvantara of fourteen, which is ruled by Vaivasvata Manu. Each Manvantara lasts for 306,720,000 years (A) and repeats seventy-one Yuga Cycles (dharmic ages). There are a total of fourteen Manvantara and fifteen Sandhikala in a Kalpa or Aeon (day of Brahmadev). Each Manvantara is followed by and the first proceeded by a period called Sandhikala. Each Sandhikala lasts for 1,728,000 (B) human years. Sandhikala is essentially the transition period during which the earth (Bhu-loka) is submerged in Garbodhaka Ocean. Thus one Day time of Operator Brahmadev constitutes 4,320,000,000 (4.32 billion) human years (=14xA+15xB). Obviously, after every Kalpa (day-time of Lord Brahma), there is a night-time of Lord Brahma too, which is known as a Brahma-Ratra. The Brahma-Ratra is of the same length as a Kalpa. Thus, one full day of Brahmadev consists of a Kalpa and a Brahma-Ratra and is 8,640,000,000 (8.64 billion) human years. This time period speaks of the creation and destruction of the universe in cycles of 8.64 billion years, which is quite close to currently accepted value regarding the time of the big bang. Is not that amazing? One of the earliest Puranas, the Vayu, conservatively dated to at least 1,500 years old, has mention of this amazing fact.

Garbodhaka Ocean: According to the Puranas, Universe is divided into two parts – One is the pure space where all planets, stars and heavenly bodies reside. Other end is at the lower end of the universe which is a celestial ocean, much like a massive black hole. That ocean is Garbodhaka Ocean.

Nandi: A childless virtuous sage named Shilada worshipped Shiva through severe penance for many years to have a boon– a special child with immortality and blessings of Shiva. Shiva granted him with his desired boon. Sage found a beautiful boy as bright as the Sun next day on his farmland while he went for ploughing. He named him Nandi, brought him up as his son with good education and wisdom. Thus Nandi is described as the son of the Sage Shilada. With his father's blessings Nandi worshipped Shiva undergoing severe penance. His great devotion and high concentration pleased Shiva. He fulfilled wishes of Nandi. Nandi became Shiva's vehicle, his doorman, his companion and head of all his ganas. Nandi got the divine-knowledge of Agamic and Tantric wisdom taught by Shiva and goddess Parvati. He taught that divine knowledge to his eight disciples, who are identified as the progenitors of Nandinatha Sampradaya viz., Sanaka, Sanatana, Sanandana, Sanatkumara, Tirumular, Vyagrapada, Patanjali and Sivayoga Muni. These eight disciples were sent in eight different directions of the world by Nandi to spread this knowledge.

Vishnunabhi: We understand the rise and fall of human consciousness in the four Yugas from the explanation given by our astronomers. They have mentioned that the Sun (with the Earth and other planets) travels along its set orbital path with its companion start, it would cyclically move close to, then away from. This oscillating point in space is referred to as *Vishnunabhi*, a supposed magnetic center or "grand center". These imply that being close to this region caused subtle changes in human consciousness that brought about the Golden Age, and conversely, our separation from it results in an age of great darkness, the Kalki Yuga.

Glossary

Veda: A Veda is a collection of poems or hymns composed in archaic Sanskrit by Indo-European-speaking peoples who lived in northwest India during the 2nd century BCE. The Vedas are a large body of religious texts (containing 20379 mantras) dealing with mantras, benedictions, rituals, ceremonies, and sacrifices originating in ancient India. Composed in Vedic Sanskrit, the texts constitute the oldest layer of Sanskrit literature and the oldest scriptures of Hinduism. There are four Vedas: the Rigveda (1500-1200 BCE), the Yajurveda, the Samaveda and the Atharvaveda (1200-900 BCE).

Upanishads: They are late Vedic Sanskrit texts of Hindu philosophy dealing with meditation, philosophy, consciousness and ontological knowledge and document a wide variety of "rites, incarnations, and esoteric knowledge" departing from Vedic ritualism and interpreted in various ways in the later commentarial traditions. The Upanishads are commonly referred to as Vedanta. There are around 108 known Upanishads of which first dozen or so are the oldest and principal Upanishads.

Puranas: These are a vast genre of Indian literature about a wide range of topics, particularly about legends and other traditional lore and are known for the intricate layers of symbolism depicted within their stories. Composed originally in Sanskrit these texts are named after major Hindu gods. Puranic literature is encyclopaedic and it includes diverse topics such as cosmogony, cosmology, genealogies of gods, goddesses, kings, heroes, sages, and demigods, folk tales, pilgrimages, temples, medicine, astronomy, grammar, mineralogy, humour, love stories, as well as theology and philosophy. The content is highly inconsistent across the Puranas and considered to be the work of many authors over the centuries. There are 18 Principal Puranas (Major Puranas) and 18 Upa Puranas (Minor Puranas), with over 400,000 verses, composed between 3rd and 10th century AD.

Primordial Inconceivable Energy: This energy is thought of as creative, sustaining, as well as destructive, and is sometimes referred to as auspicious source energy. Shakti is sometimes personified as the Creatrix, and is known as "Adi Shakti" or "Adi Para Shakti" (i.e., Primordial Inconceivable Energy).

Brahman: In Hinduism it connotes the highest universal principle, the ultimate reality in the universe. In major schools of Hindu philosophy, it is the immaterial, efficient, formal and final cause of all that exists. It is the pervasive, infinite, eternal truth, consciousness and bliss which does not change, yet is the cause of all changes. Brahman as a metaphysical concept refers to the single binding unity behind diversity in all that exists in the universe. Brahman is a Vedic Sanskrit word and it is conceptualized in Hinduism as the "creative principle which lies comprehended in the whole world. It is a key concept found in he Vedas, and it is extensively discussed in the early Upanishads. While the Vedas conceptualize Brahman as the Cosmic Principle, the Upanishads variously described it as Satchidānanda (truth-consciousness-bliss and as the unchanging, permanent, highest reality. Brahman is associated by the various philosophical schools with the concept of Atman (meaning Self, personal, impersonal or Para Brahman). As in the non-dual schools such as the Advaita Vedanta the substance of Brahman is identical to the substance of Atman and is everywhere and inside each living being and there is connected spiritual oneness in all existence. In the dualistic schools of Hinduism such as the theistic Dvaita Vedanta, Brahman is different from Atman (Self) in each being. In non-dual schools such as the Advaita, the substance of Brahman is identical to the substance of Atman, is everywhere and inside each living being, and there is connected spiritual oneness in all existence.

Acknowledgements

In my quest to produce an insight in to the mystery (mythologically wrapped) of the Centers of Divine Energy or the Shaktipeeth I depended on literatures from several sources besides my personal visits. I cited list of books, papers, journals, websites resources to trace the link of the Kanakhala mystery with the high mythological characters. Material was not necessarily used from all of these sources but many of them appeared in one article did open the doors to further research articles while studying. While citing one article only relevant references were collated. Relevant information is studied with a view to conceptualise the central theme of the novel I envisaged. In most of the Divine Centers photography was prohibited. Hence I have used a few of the images from the leaflets bought there at the centers and from some corresponding websites which I gratefully and most humbly acknowledge. This has enhanced not only the depth of the understanding but also made it more intrigued. I further acknowledge all these historical references with all humility and respects without which my work would not have been possible.

References

1. David R. Kinsley, *Hindu Goddesses: Visions of the Divine Feminine in the Hindu religious tradition,* University of California Press (1988).
2. Lynn Foulston *At the Feet of the Goddess: Divine Feminine in Local Hindu Religion*, Sussex Academic Press (1999).
3. Judith Coney, *Sahaja Yoga: Socializing Processes in a South Asian New Religious Movement* (1999)
4. C. Mackenzie Brown, *The Devi Gita: The Song of the Goddess* State University of New York Press (1998)
5. K. K. Klostermaier, *Hinduism: A Short History*, Oneworld Publication (2000).
6. Prof. Arthur Holmes *The Age of the Earth* (1913)
7. Scientist Carl Sagan *Hinduism today* (2007)
8. T R R Iyengar *Hinduism and Scientific Quest*
9. Frederic Spiegelberge *Spiritual Practices of India*
10. Horace Hayman Wilson *The Vishnu Purana: A System of Hindu Mythology and Tradition,* Punthi Pustak, 1961
11. Carl Sagan *Cosmos*, Ballantine Books, 1985
12. Rabindranath Tagore *Sadhana: The Realisation of Life*, Mau Publishing. [It is not a mere sentiment; it is truth; it is the joy that is at the root of all creation. It is the white light of pure consciousness that emanates from Brahmadev. So, to be one with this *sarvanubhuh* [Omnipotent], this all-feeling being who is in the external sky, as well ...]
13. Arvind Savant *Mandukya Upanishad: Discovery of God,* Xlibris Corporation, 2011 [Om means Brahmadev. Meaning "whole world is in this word"].

14. Agniveer *Veda*, 2013 [The Vedas were revealed by the Omniscient to four primeval Rishis; Rigveda to Agni, Yajurveda to Vayu, Sama Veda to Aditya, and Atharva Veda to Angira, directly in to their spiritual consciousness. The sage Brahmadev received and collected the four from them passed them on to other sages.]
15. Sarvapalli Radhakrishnan *Discovery of God* [Soul means Brahmadev; and the *Brhmajnan* flows through soul to the intellect. That is termed *Atmajnan*. Thus Soul (Atma), Brahmadev, and Om have same meaning].
16. Nancy Wilson Ross (1901-1986) *"Three Ways of Asian Wisdom"*, Asia Society of New York.
17. Jeffrey Armstrong *The Mysteries of Indian Culture, the Relevance of Hindu Vedas and the Reality of Ancient Flying Machines,* thedailybell.com
18. Huston Smith *The Mystic's Journey – India and the Infinite, the Soul of a people*
19. Klostermaier, Klaus K. *A Survey of Hinduism,* State University of New York (1989).
20. *Brahmadev, Encyclopedia Britannica*
21. Royina Grewal, *The Book of Ganesha,* Penguin Books India, 2009
22. Ganga Mahatya, Devdutt Pattanaik, Penguin Books India, 2008.
23. Salil Gewali *Great Minds on India*, Penguin Random House (2013), New Delhi
24. Ambrose Bierce, *The Devil's Dictionary* (1911)
25. Catherine Benton *God of Desire: Tales of Kamadeva*, Sunny Press, 2006
26. Shantha N. Nair *Echoes of Ancient Indian Wisdom: The Universal Hindu Vision and Its Edifice*, Pustak Mahal, 2008.

27. Philosophies of India by Heinrich Zimmer, Princeton University Press (1969).
28. "The Wishing Tree" by Subhash Kak.
29. Shri 108 & Other Mysteries and the Cycle of Time by Subhash Kak.
30. Galactic Alignment – By John Major Jenkins.
31. Rig Veda – translated by Ralph Griffith.

The End

www.ingramcontent.com/pod-product-compliance
Lightning Source LLC
LaVergne TN
LVHW041158150826
845673LV00001B/202

* 9 7 9 8 8 9 1 8 6 5 0 9 9 *